PRAISE FOR
LATE TO YOUR OWN FUNERAL

"Rachel Donnelly's *Late to Your Own Funeral* is not just about estate planning; it's about information stewardship. It highlights the importance of preserving, organizing, and transmitting essential knowledge so that those left behind are empowered, not overwhelmed. Estate transitions are not merely about legal documents and financial assets—they are about the preservation of personal histories, digital footprints, and practical guidance that smooth the path for loved ones navigating life without us.

In a world where an increasing amount of our lives is stored in encrypted digital realms, the question of access is as critical as the assets themselves. How will your family retrieve essential records, manage your unfinished business, or maintain the continuity of your intentions if they are left in the dark? This book challenges us to face the often-avoided task of preparing our affairs with clarity and foresight, ensuring that our information does not become an unsolvable puzzle but a well-marked roadmap.

Rachel approaches this difficult topic with humor, honesty, and a wealth of practical strategies that transform estate planning from a dreaded chore into an act of love. Whether it's a lifetime of financial records, the passwords to critical accounts, or simply the stories that define who we are, *Late to Your Own Funeral* teaches us that taking control of our information today spares our loved ones the burden of untying the knots of uncertainty tomorrow."

Nathaniel Robinson, Founder & CEO of Trustworthy.com

"This is the book we all need, but don't necessarily want to think about. *Late to Your Own Funeral* is equal parts hilarious, heartfelt, and brutally honest . . . A guide to facing life's biggest certainty with clarity, organization, and even a little laughter."

Adam Zuckerman, Founder of Buried in Work

"In *Late To Your Own Funeral,* Rachel Donnelly masterfully combines sound estate planning advice with humor and real-life stories of estate planning (or the lack thereof). As a professional in after loss care for 15 years, I discovered new strategies I need to incorporate with my clients! This book is really a must-read for everyone—unless you can guarantee you won't die!"

Shane Phillips, author of *First Steps: A Comprehensive Guide to Financial Matters After a Death*

"We are all storytellers, whether we realize it or not. Our legacy isn't just the assets we leave behind—it's the conversations we have and the lives we touch. *Late to Your Own Funeral* is a wake-up call for anyone who believes that avoiding the conversation will somehow delay the inevitable. Rachel Donnelly masterfully turns estate planning from a daunting task into an act of love, making planning for the inevitable less about paperwork and more about purpose—ensuring that our final chapter reflects the life we truly lived. Planning ahead is the best way to leave a legacy of love—not just legal battles—and Donnelly's wisdom makes that process both meaningful and manageable."

Roy U. Moëd, Founder & CEO of LifeBook Memoirs

"*Late to Your Own Funeral* invites all of us in—whether you're wondering, 'What's the least I can do?' or you're the super achiever ready to lock in every detail of a life well lived and planned. Read it until you uncover that first action item, do it, and return when you're ready for more. The book will invite you back in and keep you engaged with humor that only a Southern belle can deliver.

Many of us walk the Earth with vague ideas of what we should do to prepare for our inevitable demise, but few of us take action. *Late to Your Own Funeral* lays out the must-dos of estate planning and all the accessories to get through the uncomfortable, awkward, and often painful steps we tend to avoid. Let this book be your guide to being prepared—even if never fully ready—for the inevitable, with a sense of humor and grace along the way."

Ellen Goodwin, Co-Founder & CSO of Artifcts

"As an estate planning professional for twenty years, I sat down to read a chapter or two of *Late to Your Own Funeral* and could not help finishing the book in one sitting. This book does what I always strive to do for my clients; it covers what is otherwise a gloomy and taboo subject in an approachable way, making a meaningful case as to why estate planning isn't optional for anyone. This easy-to-read how-to (and why-to) book should mysteriously appear on your parents' nightstand to give them an entertaining, engaging push to put their affairs in order. A hilarious and informative must-read for anyone who is mortal!"

Abbey Flaum, J.D., LL.M., estate planning attorney

"As a financial advisor, I know how complex and tedious the administrative work can be after losing a loved one. Rachel has the gift of making the uncomfortable funny. You will be laughing out loud while simultaneously taking notes. This is one of those nonfiction books that is easy to ready because she has weaved so many stories and personal experiences into the information. Almost everyone is unprepared for the work involved in dealing with an estate. This book is a must read."

Charlotte C. Geletka, CFP, CRPC

"What I love about Rachel is she gets right to the point and doesn't waste anyone's time and this book is no exception. This is the resource for figuring out everything you need to know quickly when you have no time to waste!"

Miles Adams, Co-Founder and CEO of Oaktree Memorials and former Head of Operations at Tulip Cremation

"Full of the wit and wisdom that is Rachel Donnelly. Before or after the death of a loved one, she helps us sort through all the necessary stuff with her smarts, experience, efficiency, compassion, and a sense of humor."

Jennifer A. O'Brien, MSOD, award-winning author of *The Hospice Doctor's Widow* and *Care Boss*

"Rachel Donnelly deftly navigates the complexities of legacy planning in *Late To Your Own Funeral*, providing invaluable guidance with both warmth and wisdom. A must-read for anyone looking to ease the administrative burdens of death."

Suzanne O'Brien, RN, author of *The Good Death*

"A must-read for anyone who wants to spare their loved ones unnecessary stress, expense, and confusion! This book offers clear, practical guidance with wit and compassion to prepare your estate the right way.

Smart, compassionate, and incredibly useful—this book is the ultimate roadmap for organizing your affairs and giving your family the gift of preparedness.

An invaluable guide to getting your estate in order before it's too late. Practical, thorough, and essential reading for anyone who cares about their legacy.

No one likes to think about death, but failing to plan can leave your loved ones overwhelmed. Rachel Donnelly makes estate planning accessible, actionable, and even empowering.

If you think estate planning is just for the wealthy, think again. This book shows why preparing now is one of the greatest acts of love you can give your family."

Ed Michael Reggie, Founder and CEO of Funeralocity

"I had no idea if I should scream, cry, or laugh. This book delivers the comedy and tragedy of death in the modern day. *Late to Your Own Funeral* engages and propels the reader through the unknown of death with gallows humor and sparkling quips."

Jason Zamer, TGBeyond

"As Donnelly states: '10 out of 10 of us will die in our lifetime.' This book is a necessary, funny, and practical guide that emphasizes the importance of organizing your affairs to ease the burden on loved ones after death. Unlike traditional books on estate planning, Donnelly focuses on the human element by weaving in personal anecdotes and reflections—encouraging readers to be mindful of the mess they could leave behind. The book is a blend of humor, wisdom, and compassion, making a heavy subject feel approachable and doable!

This book is an excellent starting point for anyone looking to minimize future chaos during a time of grief for their loved ones. It pairs well with more formal estate planning and inspires readers to take proactive steps to leave a legacy of love and simplicity, rather than unnecessary clutter."

Tiffany N. McKenzie, Esq., estate planning attorney

"*Late for Your Own Funeral* is a funny and entertaining book about a subject that is not particularly funny or entertaining. Rachel cusses like a sailor in a brothel—not that we know what this sounds like—as she regales us with stories of administrative nightmares in the wake of loved ones dying without a will or estate plan. If you thought that the only certain things in life were death and taxes, you can potentially add one more: the dumpster fire you need to clean up when a close relative dies. If you are looking to be scared straight when it comes to organizing your affairs before you die, *Late for Your Own Funeral* is the book for you."

Barry Koch, TGBeyond

"From Rachel's heartfelt stories and her unmatchable wit, this book is a remarkable invitation to get your legacy in order. The honest stories of real people who place their loved ones in a financial nightmare will empower the reader to embrace this guidebook of practical steps to take now. Rachel's life, loss, and mission to help others through life's most difficult times is inspiring, thoughtful, and compelling. This book and its author will become your new best friend to share with others."

Kathi Balasek, CEO of Grief Smart Professional

"*Late To Your Own Funeral* is an absolute must-read. Period. Rachel masterfully blends practical advice and insightful education with real-life stories—and yes, a refreshing dose of humor—because, let's be honest, even life's most serious matters can have their comedic moments.

Estate planning and settling affairs are often seen as concerns reserved for the elderly or the ultra-wealthy, but this book completely upends that misconception. Rachel makes it clear: planning ahead isn't just for a select few—it's for everyone. No matter your stage in life, you'll leave this book with a newfound understanding of why estate planning matters and, more importantly, how to make the process easier for yourself and those you love.

Engaging, informative, and unexpectedly funny, *Late To Your Own Funeral* transforms an often-overlooked topic into an essential conversation. Do yourself—and your loved ones—a favor: read this book."

Tara Faquir, Co-Founder and
Chief Operating Officer of Trustate

LATE TO YOUR OWN FUNERAL

LATE TO YOUR OWN FUNERAL

How To Leave a Legacy and Not a Logjam

Rachel Balog Donnelly

Published by Ripples Media
www.ripples.media

Copyright © 2025 by Rachel Balog Donnelly

First printing 2025

Cover design & book interior by Carolyn Asman

ISBN 979-8-9925127-0-0 Paperback
ISBN 979-8-9925127-1-7 Hardback
ISBN 979-8-9925127-2-4 E-book

DEDICATION

To my mom, dad, and Uncle G—thank you for providing both the inspiration for this book and plenty to unpack in therapy.

To Zack, Finn, and Roane—Team Donnelly forever.

To all the executors and soon-to-be executors out there—you're the unsung heroes of life's hardest moments.

To my clients—thank you for placing your trust in me during such personal and challenging times.

And to death—thank you for shaping my perspective and becoming an unexpected part of my journey.

CONTENTS

FOREWORD

When I first heard about Rachel Donnelly's mission to help people organize their legacies, I felt an immediate kinship. Like Rachel, my journey into this field wasn't planned. It was forged through loss. In a span of just eighteen months, I lost my father, stepfather, and both grandfathers. Grief became a central part of my life, and I realized that navigating the practical aftermath of death—sorting through belongings, managing estates, and organizing memories—was a job that no one ever really prepares you for.

It's the job that sucks, as my grandfather used to say, but it's also the job that matters. And, as he wisely told me when I was a kid: "If something sucks, you need to do that as a job because people will pay you to do it." That advice shaped my life's work, and it's why Rachel's approach resonates so deeply with me.

In *Late To Your Own Funeral*, Rachel takes on this uncomfortable, often-avoided topic with wit, compassion, and brutal honesty. Her irreverent humor and no-nonsense guidance make legacy planning not just manageable but oddly enjoyable. It's that mix of humor and honesty that is hard to find at the moment that it's needed. She helps readers confront the chaos of "what happens next," transforming it into a thoughtful gift for those left behind.

This isn't just a book about estate planning or organizing your stuff. It's about finding clarity in chaos and creating a roadmap for your loved ones when you're no longer here to guide them. Rachel doesn't shy away from the hard truths, and she'll make you laugh even as you're squirming in discomfort. Her straightforward approach cuts through the discomfort, encouraging empowerment through proactive planning.

I've always believed that the most important work we do is born out of our own challenges. Rachel's personal experiences have shaped her into a true expert in this field. She understands what it means to be overwhelmed by loss, and she's turned that understanding into a lifeline for others. Anyone who has made helping people with grief a career will tell you that challenges are opportunities to help someone. This book is a must-read for anyone looking to make sense of the complexities that follow death. It's an invitation to tackle one of life's most challenging moments with grace and foresight.

So, dive in. Laugh, learn, and start creating the legacy that only you can leave. Because the truth is, none of us are getting out of here alive. But we can leave behind something beautiful and organized for those who matter most.

Matt Paxton
Author of *Keep the Memories, Lose the Stuff*
& host of *Hoarders and Filthy Fortunes*

INTRODUCTION

"Well, they found a tumor in my chest the size of Chicago," my mother said. She always did have a way with words, even when the topic was dark. When she said it, her voice cracked a little, and I could tell she was scared. My mother wasn't scared of anything until now.

I was sitting in my new closet. We had moved into the house days before. I was organizing my clothes for a new job I was starting the following week. I could hear my one- and four-year-old kids downstairs with my husband playing with their toys in the new living room. Everything felt new and exciting, but this pulled me out of the clouds and into reality.

The familiar dread settled in my stomach. "Not again," I whispered to the silent room, memories of my father's cancer battle flashing through my mind. The future loomed with hospital visits, surgeries, and chemo—a rerun of past pains at a time when I was busier than ever.

In just sixty days, my world flipped. My mom was diagnosed, underwent a nine-hour surgery, and died. Suddenly, I was not only navigating a new job with no paid time off but also managing my Uncle Granville's care, who was battling late-stage Parkinson's Disease 900 miles away, without any direct support. What ensued was a labyrinth of caregiving overwhelm, probate, estate administration, and seemingly endless house cleanouts.

If you've ever seen that meme with the dog sitting in his chair, sipping coffee, and telling himself, "This is fine," while the room around him is ablaze in flames, that's about how I felt.

WHY THIS BOOK MATTERS AND A LEGAL DISCLAIMER

Death, as inevitable and universal as it is, comes with a bag of uncertainties and unspoken rules. Aside from it being completely sad and heartbreaking, nobody ever seems to know what the eff to do.

This isn't just a book; it's a survival guide written from my perspective as an after loss professional and someone who's been in the trenches of death's bureaucracy. I like to say that I've graduated from the school of hard knocks with an MDA—a Master's in Death Administration—and I've written this book to be a roadmap and step-by-step guide out of estate settlement purgatory.

This book is about death and dying, surviving the loss of a loved one, estate administration gone wrong, and coming out on the other side of closing their Xfinity account. While the business of death or logistics will vary from country to country and state to state, this book is meant to provide a methodology and approach to getting your affairs in order, which I refer to as legacy planning.

So, what's legacy planning? Imagine it as a cocktail mixed with one part organization, one part strategy, a dash of your hopes and dreams, and a generous pour of adulting—yes, that means pulling up your big-girl pants and dealing with your mess. It's your life, your legacy, so don't expect anyone else to sort through what you want, read your mind, or decide the fate of your cherished Hummel figurine collection.

This book is meant to not only help you get organized and plan ahead but also to help whatever poor soul will be your executor. Technically, an executor is a person or institution appointed by a testator (a person who has written a Will) to carry out the terms of their Will. However, in this book, just know that we're using the term executor generally to mean whoever is in charge of settling your estate.

Full disclosure: This book is no substitute for expert professional advice. Let's be clear—I'm not an attorney, a financial advisor, or an accountant, and flipping through these pages won't magically make you one, either. The advice and stories shared here are drawn from my estate administration escapades in the State of Georgia, which might not translate directly to your neck of the woods. I urge you not to go rogue with just this book in hand! Always consult with experienced professionals. The information provided here is intended for informational amusement and enlightenment only and should not be mistaken for comprehensive financial, funeral, legal, medical, or tax advice.

Furthermore, this book is for the average Gen Pop American with a typical estate. If you're in the 1%, own a jet, have offshore accounts, and a house in Monaco, this might not be your playbook. But chances are, you've got a battalion of advisors for that. For the rest of us mere mortals—welcome to your guide through the last great adventure.

So now that we've covered what I'm not, let me tell you what I am: an after loss professional. You're probably wondering, "What in the hell is an after loss professional?" I'm so glad you asked.

An after loss professional is a specialist who provides comprehensive logistical and administrative support to individuals after a death, usually those appointed as executors or administrators of an estate following a loved one's death. We offer personalized guidance to help clients navigate the complex responsibilities that come with managing an estate, ensuring that nothing is overlooked. By integrating a broad overview of all tasks required, after loss professionals bridge the gaps left by other professionals' more specialized or fragmented roles, offering a holistic approach to estate management. This ensures that clients receive the support they need to fulfill their duties effectively and with less stress. If you're still scratching your head, some people have described us like wedding coordinators, but for death.

After my mom died, I was on the struggle bus big time. Hell, I felt like I was driving the struggle bus. I had just moved into a new house, had two small children, and just started a new job, which, as we all know, is the time to really wow your new boss. I was barely keeping it together—let alone impressing anyone.

It's hard enough starting a new job and attempting to learn all of the new procedures, your colleague's names, the organizational hierarchy, who to report to, the politics, and how to get things done. I essentially had two new jobs: one that paid me and one that didn't, the latter of which was my new role as an executor. I tried to toe the line, but at one point, I just couldn't do it anymore. After eight months of driving the struggle bus, I decided to pull off and take time out to settle my mom's estate and get my uncle's affairs in order.

In the back of my mind, I wished I had someone to help me. I wished I had some kind of a personal assistant to help me get organized. I needed help to keep track of the paperwork going in and out. I also wished for help finding the professionals I needed and understanding the mysterious world of probate. There wasn't anyone.

Little did I know that one day, I would create the profession that I needed myself. They say that necessity is the mother of invention, so I created a role now known as an after loss professional. This role, which would have been a lifesaver in my time of need, serves as a project manager to clients. I help them manage the avoidable logistics and administrative tasks of death through one-on-one support.

It took time, trial and error, and finding others in this space to curate what we now call the after loss profession. What has emerged is a budding niche industry aimed at helping others through one of the worst times of their lives. There's a "misery loves company" joke somewhere in there.

Before we move on, *I want to make clear that this book is not meant to make light of the intense experience of death*. Losing those we love sucks. Death is tragic, life-altering, devastating, and just plain sad. Death is one of the most human of human experiences and one that we can't avoid.

It's ironic, really. Death is the most human of experiences, yet it's the one event that consistently catches us off guard. This book is about changing that narrative. It's about preparing for the inevitable with grace and foresight so that when the time comes, mourning isn't overshadowed by administrative nightmares.

Because we don't know what to do or where to even start after someone dies, we are robbed of our grief process. This leaves us emotionally stunted and robbed of the crucial grieving that helps us heal. Instead, we're stuck on hold with American Express, pausing Netflix accounts, and figuring out how to shut down Facebook pages—it's like being stuck in customer service purgatory when we should be mourning.

When I experienced loss, I didn't want another GD Honey-baked Ham or sour cream pound cake. What I needed, and what many need, is practical help. I was so impacted by these experiences that they led me to create my after loss services and my company, AfterLight. My goal in writing this book is to give you the tools and processes for when this process happens as well as to demonstrate how critical it is for you and your family to do the prep work, as awkward and uncomfortable as it may initially seem so that you're not left with a flaming dumpster fire.

CHAPTER 01
THE BUSINESS OF DEATH: THE FLAMING DUMPSTER FIRE WE LEAVE IN OUR WAKE

"Granville, you could f**k up a two-car funeral," my mother yelled into her cell phone, her Southern accent thick as molasses. Her voice was filled with utter and complete exasperation. My mother had a saying for everything, and, to her, cussing was an art form, and the spoken word was her canvas.

Growing up, whenever my mother unleashed this particular idiom, I'd puzzle over it, imagining the logistics of a two-car funeral. Surely, one car would be the hearse, right? How could that possibly go awry? For those unfamiliar, this saying suggests that the person in question is so incompetent they'd botch even the simplest task.

At that moment, we were at the hospital together for her pre-op meeting with the surgical team, preparing for the daunting nine-hour procedure to remove the aforementioned Chicago-sized tumor from her chest.

As the words flew from her mouth, I buried my face in my hands, cringing. Her choice of words felt particularly harsh, given my uncle's deteriorating health. Suffering from Parkinson's Disease, he was showing signs of significant cognitive decline. But my mother, facing her mortality, lashed out in fear more than malice as she scrambled to help update her brother Granville's financial power of attorney and health-care directives in case the surgery went south.

Sadly, it did. She never left the hospital and died just a few weeks later.

Her biggest fear had been dying and leaving us to manage her affairs and care for my uncle. Now, as I reflect on managing my uncle's care in the late stages of Parkinson's, I realize it paled in comparison to the complexities of settling my mother's estate.

Life is messy. But death? That can be even messier, especially when it comes to the business of death.

You're probably wondering what I mean by the "business of death." No, it's not some creepy, behind-the-scenes enterprise. I'm talking about the unavoidable administrative nightmare that is unwinding a person's life after they kick the bucket. Think about it: from the moment we pop into the world, we start leaving a trail of all kinds of stuff—both physical and digital. And boy, does that trail get longer and messier as time goes on.

Every time you sign up for a new streaming service, open a bank account, or even just buy another gizmo for your ever-growing collection, you're adding to your life's footprint. This footprint doesn't just vanish when you shuffle off this mortal coil. Nope, it sticks around, waiting for someone to come along and sort it all out. And guess who gets that job? Yep, your grieving loved ones.

Picture this: your family, already neck-deep in Kleenex, now has to dive into stacks of paperwork, try to track down your financial mysteries, and navigate the Wild West of your digital life. As my mama would say, it's like trying to nail Jell-O to the wall. Not fun.

My first experience with the business of death was when my father died when I was sixteen. My sister was six weeks away from graduating from high school, and my brother was fourteen. There's never a good time to die, but my father's illness and death happened during a phase of a lot of changes for my siblings and me.

My father's death introduced me to learning about the business of death, the first lesson being that when someone dies, you've got to fill out a lot of forms. It felt as though I had to turn in a death punch card in exchange for money and benefits from the government. That process wasn't simple whatsoever. It was insanely bureaucratic and confusing. Since my father was a Vietnam War veteran, I was now eligible for Social Security Administration benefits as a dependent under eighteen and Veterans Administration benefits. My mother took care of the Social Security benefits, given that I was under eighteen, but during my senior year in high school, when I turned eighteen, I needed to complete the forms myself.

I still have PTSD from filling out all of those VA forms. It was painful. The forms had to be filled out in writing and faxed in—yes, faxed in. I remember counting over forty-five pages at one time and having to do this every couple of months to prove that I was still in school and that I still needed the money. I would then have to call and spend hours on hold waiting for someone at the VA to tell me whether they received it or not.

Who knew this exercise would prepare me for my career as an after loss professional because I became a champion at yelling "REPRESENTATIVE"?

I usually receive calls from potential clients in the first few days or weeks following their loved one's death. It is fresh. It is raw. And nine times out of ten, they have no idea what they should be doing. They don't know what they don't know. Yes, they understand that they have to notify family and friends, plan a funeral, and write an obituary, but what happens beyond that is clear as mud.

One of my first clients as a newly practicing after loss professional was David, the son of a Vietnam Veteran who had died of COVID very early in the pandemic. A friend had purchased one of my In Lieu of Flowers packages for them to help in the early days of the loss of their father. David's mother was left devastated by his father's death, not only because she had lost her husband but because he had received VA benefits that greatly supplemented their income. Now that he had died, the benefits ended.

This felt like it was right up my alley, helping the widow and children of a Vietnam veteran, taking on this behemoth of a governmental agency once again. I cracked my knuckles, gave myself a pat on the back, and dug into the paperwork. Surprisingly, the VA has made some changes for the better in terms of giving more information to veterans and their families.

In my day, I had to mail off for a booklet, waiting weeks for its arrival, only to tear into some masterpiece entitled something like *Your Dead Veteran and You* and to be left scratching my head on whether or not you qualified.

Unfortunately, I was able to find out pretty quickly that David's mother would not qualify for any benefits moving forward. I called an attorney I had worked with before who was an expert in VA benefits, and she confirmed what I already knew. Even though this was disappointing to David and his mother, it gave him the information he needed to make decisions to move forward. I helped David with other aspects of settling his dad's affairs, and then he was on his way.

When we leave this earth, someone is left behind to execute a laundry list of tasks ranging from what may be crystal clear to completely unknown. What I mean by that is if we don't plan ahead, executors are left to put together a breadcrumb trail in settling their loved one's affairs. Regardless of whether it is straightforward or not, the business death task list that unfurls when someone dies is insane. To make matters worse, those who are left behind are grieving you.

According to Wired.com, the question "What do you do when someone dies?" is typed into Google by more than a hundred million people each month. This means that a lot of people are confused AF.

Remember that old Jerry Seinfeld bit about America's greatest fears, with public speaking ranking first and death second? This, of course, means that people would rather be in the casket than giving the eulogy. The corollary to this is that some could argue you're better off dead than to be an executor of an estate. Welcome to the business of death.

——— ⚰ ———

WHAT NEEDS TO BE DONE WHEN SOMEONE DIES

There can be over one hundred tasks to be completed after someone dies. To help orient you in the business of death, here's a crash course on what must be taken care of when someone dies:

Immediate First Steps
- Call a funeral home to make arrangements.
- Arrange care for dependents and pets.
- Secure homes and vehicles, gather keys, and change locks where needed.
- Plan a funeral, memorial, or celebration of life.
- If possible, ensure mortgages and any other critical bills, such as insurance, continue to be paid to prevent foreclosure or lapses in coverage.

Notification, Documentation, & Organization
- Obtain ten to fifteen original copies of the death certificate.
- Gather important documents and information (personal documents, debts, assets, Will, and/or Trust documents).
- Notify relevant agencies and organizations such as the Social Security office, Veterans Affairs, the landlord, and the decedent's employer.
- Notify the attorney, financial advisor, accountant, and/or other professionals.

Opening the Estate
- Retain an attorney to review the Will and/or Trust and advise on the appropriate steps for estate administration.

- Determine the best path forward for opening and managing the estate, including filing for Administration of Estate or Probate of Will, if necessary.
- Marshal assets, determine ownership and clarify direct beneficiary designations.
- Take inventory of the decedent's belongings and tangible personal property.
- Keep track of any outstanding debts or bills.
- Issue a Notice to Debtors and Creditors.
- Notify and communicate with the heirs and beneficiaries about the estate proceedings.

Estate Administration
- Consult with an attorney or CPA about managing and distributing retirement accounts, ensuring compliance with tax laws and beneficiary designations.
- Close, transfer, and/or archive accounts, including digital ones.
- Secure and enforce life insurance policies and payouts.
- Continue to pay essential bills, like the mortgage, to prevent foreclosure.
- Liquidate tangible personal property if necessary.
- Clean out and prepare to sell any real estate properties.
- Resolve outstanding debts and retrieve any funds owed to the decedent.
- Submit both state and federal tax returns for the estate, as well as any required individual tax returns.
- Allocate assets and property as dictated to the estate plan or state law.

Close Estate
- Cover final expenses such as attorney fees, reimburse the executor, and distribute the remaining estate.

- Officially discharge the executor and close the estate.

Are you exhausted just looking at this list? Yeah, join the club. If they ever do a remake of *Mr. Smith Goes to Washington,* and the junior senator needs to stand in front of the chamber and filibuster for several minutes, maybe he should read this task list. This may only be a straightforward path if your loved one has done some planning ahead of time. Meaning that it will be a lot easier if you are able to access documents, have some idea of what your loved one wants, etc. That doesn't mean it's easy. Even with a "straightforward" estate, the logistical and administrative tasks still lie ahead. And they are daunting, to say the least.

------ ❢ ------

SIMPLIFYING ESTATE ADMINISTRATION

To me, the estate administration process can be simplified into the following steps:

Notify

Notify family, friends, employer, funeral home, locksmith, alarm company, attorney, financial advisor, beneficiaries, banks, insurance company, etc. You get the gist. These days, you'll feel like the telephone operator at the Home Shopping Network—always on call and always explaining.

Organize and Marshal

Now you have to play detective to find everything: paperwork, statements, and accounts. This includes what they owned and what they owed while at the same time figuring out how to access funds to pay for funeral arrangements and immediate expenses.

You'll need to create a spreadsheet of everything and keep track of your expenses. Your weekends are now spent sorting through decades of tax returns, finding online accounts you never knew existed, and explaining to relatives why a teapot is not part of their inheritance.

Administer

Once you have the legal authority as executor or administrator, you can start closing, transferring, and/or retitling the estate assets according to the estate plan or attorney's directions. You'll also have to make a million decisions and settle disputes of who gets Grandma's pie plate, all while dodging phone calls from Xfinity.

Distribute

Once the estate has been administered and the attorney gives the green light, it's time to handle the final affairs: pay all outstanding bills, file any necessary individual and/or estate tax returns, distribute assets to beneficiaries, and reimburse yourself as executor. After potentially months or years and about 500 hours of effort, you can finally see reimbursement or even payment for this colossal second job you've undertaken.

Close

Once all that is done, you can close the estate. You'll receive a discharge from the probate court as the executor which will be the best feeling ever. Do a little jig. It's over.

Note: These steps are typical for a "traditional" uncontested estate. If disputes arise and attorneys get involved on all sides, brace for a longer, more complicated process. Throughout, you'll make an inordinate number of phone calls that feel like advanced levels of bureaucratic hell. You'll often need to provide a death certificate and proof of your executor status multiple times, and despite the hyperbole, the process can feel as intrusive as a blood and urine test. Each call may bring different answers, timelines, or requirements, adding layers of frustration to an already daunting task.

— ⚰ —

LOCKED OUT AND LEFT BEHIND

I once had a client, Shannon, who had lost her brother Blake unexpectedly to COVID. Blake wasn't married, didn't have children, and was a solopreneur who lived alone. Shannon and Blake were not only brother and sister, but they were best friends. Shannon was gutted by the loss of her brother. To make matters worse, she had no idea about her brother's finances or business affairs. She was locked out of Blake's phone and computer because she didn't know his unlock code or password. Shannon was very emotional about the loss of her brother and the lack of information she had on hand. She would often break down in tears of exasperation and grief.

We found out that Blake had multiple personal and business checking accounts at various financial institutions, and one day, called one of the institutions to ask about closing and transferring the account funds to the estate. With Shannon on the phone with me to provide verification, I explained the situation in detail to the representative on the other line and told her what we were hoping to do. After verifying several details, the representative asked to speak with Blake.

I was floored. I just couldn't believe it. I was terrified that Shannon was going to erupt in a breakdown any second, which would have been completely understandable. The sad thing is that this has happened multiple times with many estates that I've helped with. Can I get an amen that representatives and financial institutions need more training around how to deal with affairs like this?

I once had two clients, Mara and Natalie, who called me within a few days of their mom dying after a long battle with cancer. Mara was a middle school teacher who had taken some time off to take care of their mother at the end of her life. Her sister, Natalie, was a full-time mom, raising her son while also sharing the responsibility of taking care of their mother as she received hospice care.

Mara and Natalie had been referred to me by a death doula, a professional who assists in the dying process, which made me feel relieved that they had received that level of support when their mom was actively dying. They were overwhelmed and had no idea where to start.

Thankfully, their mom had a Will and had been clear about her wishes after she was gone. Their mom had been living with Natalie when she died but still had her own house as well as a mountain house, which Mara and Natalie wanted to keep.

When their mom died, Mara and Natalie were devastated. Their father had died several years before, and the prospect of facing the many decisions and administrative tasks on their own felt paralyzing.

Some of their initial questions were:

- What bills do we pay and in what order, including the medical bills?
- Should we continue to pay the mortgage while we figure all of this out?
- How do we transfer the mountain house into our names?
- Do we need an attorney?
- Can we keep her car?

After introducing Mara, the designated executor, to an attorney to initiate the probate process, Mara and I began dealing with the mortgage company about possibly assuming the loan on the mountain house. We spent countless hours on the phone, enduring a frustrating cycle of transfers to different company departments, receiving inconsistent information, and repeatedly being asked to have Mara's mom join the call. It was an exhausting and mind-numbing experience.

— ⚰ —

LIFE DOESN'T STOP, EVEN FOR DEATH

One of the hardest realities to wrap your mind around when someone dies is that life continues on. The carousel doesn't stop for you to hop off, take a break, have a total breakdown, take care of shit, and then get back on. Much to our disbelief, it keeps moving.

On the way home from the hospital after my father died, our car broke down for the 900th time. God bless that blue Dodge Caravan with faux wood paneling and an overly aggressive sliding door that would take your fingers off if they got in the way. Here we are, sitting on the side of I-75 southbound in downtown Atlanta, broken down just a few hours after my father had died. This was 1995, so the cell phone options were limited, but somehow, my mother managed to call my dad's answering service, and the owner came and picked us up.

I have a vivid memory of being stuffed in the back of a red Isuzu Rodeo while my grandmother tried to diffuse the situation by rummaging through her purse and offering up days-old, lint-covered peanut butter crackers. I remember being furious when she asked if I wanted GD peanut butter crackers. I mean, how could I possibly eat after watching my father die just a short few hours before?

Fast forward many years later to the day of my mom's funeral. I was trying to dress my two-year-old daughter in a black dress and tights, which is like trying to put socks on a rooster, when I heard water rushing down the hallway. My uncle had been in the bathroom for way too long, and I heard him exclaim, "Oh no." I heard a dreaded gush of water down the hall. My uncle, bless his heart and diminishing faculties, had turned the bathroom and adjacent hallway into an indoor fountain. Just perfect, the absolute cherry on top of an already overwhelming day.

Now, take a moment to think about your life—your daily schedule, the endless juggling of tasks. Picture adding estate sorting to that circus. Without simple planning tools in place, like knowing whether your loved one had a Will or where they kept their financial documents, the circus turns into outright pandemonium.

Remember, getting your affairs in order isn't just about you. It's about sparing your family the headache of sorting through your chaos while they're not only reeling from your loss but also trying to keep all those plates spinning as the world relentlessly moves forward. Because life won't pause for your departure, I assure you. By taking the time to address this now, you're offering them the ultimate gift: the ability to grieve without having to wade through a swamp of administrative muck.

CHAPTER 02
WHAT HAPPENS AFTER:
WHEN YOU DON'T DO SHIT

If you haven't done any planning, you're in good company—unfortunately. A recent Caring.com survey reveals a scary trend: 76% of Americans are without a Will. So, only 24% of U.S. adults have a Will, a number that has steadily decreased from 33% in 2022. Moreover, only 13% of Americans have a Trust, and an overwhelming 56% have absolutely nothing in the form of an estate plan—zilch, nada. What are the most popular excuses? "I haven't gotten around to it," followed by "I don't have enough assets to leave to anyone."

However, the size of your assets doesn't dictate the need for an estate plan. Contrary to popular belief, less wealth doesn't mean less complexity when the Grim Reaper comes calling. In fact, the more modest your means, the more tangled the web can become.

A sage attorney once put it succinctly: "Your estate is not just what you own, but also what you owe." Without a plan, separating assets from debts can turn into an epic saga.

One of the most frustrating things I hear people say is, "My estate is simple," which implies that they either don't need to do any planning or only need to do the bare minimum. My follow-up question to them is, "Simple for whom?" It might seem straightforward to you, but your idea of "simple" could be a complex puzzle for those you leave behind. Sometimes, the seemingly most straightforward task can end up taking the longest, with or without an estate plan.

Here's the kicker: if you don't make a Will, the state steps in to create one for you, following a set of rules known as "intestate succession" laws. While each state has its own variations, the goal remains the same: to distribute your estate in a standardized manner that presumably reflects common familial priorities. However, despite their attempts to be uniformly applicable, these laws may not align with your personal wishes or accurately represent your family dynamics.

Picture this: you're single, no kids, and you haven't seen your globetrotting dad, who is on his sixth wife in a decade. You could die without a Will, and surprise—your estranged dad could be splitting your assets with your mom. That's the state, playing matchmaker in the afterlife. In other words, the choices the law makes for you might not always line up with what you would have wanted.

While losing your assets to the wrong hands is bad, it's just the tip of the iceberg. The real chaos unfolds when your lack of planning lights up a fiery mess of legal delays, financial strains, and family feuds. Who wants their legacy to be a family brawl and a pile of paperwork?

The list of problems that could ensue is lengthy, and while it's tempting to delve into each, I'll spare you the exhaustive rundown and focus on some of the most critical concerns. These top-line issues could ignite a veritable flaming dumpster fire of complications for your family if you die unprepared:

ISSUE ONE:

YOUR MINOR CHILDREN COULD BE COMPLETELY AND TOTALLY SCREWED

I know this isn't something anyone wants to consider, but imagine what would happen if you and your spouse or partner died simultaneously without any estate planning.

Now, not only are your kids grappling with the unimaginable loss of both parents, but they're also thrust into a legal and emotional tornado.

If you have minor children, leaving them without a Will is akin to leaving them wandering unsupervised in the Trader Joe's parking lot.

Without a Will, the court decides who will take care of your kids. Yes, strangers in robes make that call, and they might not choose the person you would have. Grandma? Your best friend? That cool aunt who believes Oreos are a well-rounded breakfast? The judge might have other ideas. And without sugarcoating it, the last thing your grieving children need is a custody battle straight out of *The Young and the Restless*.

But wait, it gets worse. The uncertainty of who will raise your kids is compounded by the daunting task of managing whatever assets you leave behind for them. Without clear instructions, the court appoints a guardian for the estate—someone who may be clueless about handling money. Even if they are competent, they're burdened with navigating endless bureaucratic hoops while trying to comfort your children.

Here's another heartbreaker: imagine if you're divorced and your ex-spouse dies, leaving minor children. A friend of mine, who's an estate attorney, had a client with two-year-old twins. Her ex-husband died without a Will, and despite being the twins' mother and legal guardian, the court limited her access to their inheritance to the bare minimum. The result? She's financially handcuffed, struggling to provide for her children beyond basic needs—truly a parent's worst nightmare.

My parents never flew together because they feared a freak plane crash, leaving my siblings and me as real-life Little Orphan Annies. In retrospect, it was totally irrational since you're more likely to die in a car crash than a plane crash, but that didn't stop them from driving all over Georgia in my daddy's blue Caddy.

Suppose your sister steps up to take care of your kids. Great, right? Except now she has to deal with the financial mess you left. Every expense for your kids must be justified and documented to the court. Need money for soccer camp? You'd better have a lawyer on speed dial. Sorting out the college fund? Good luck doing that without any clear instructions.

Oh, and did I mention the potential for family drama? Imagine your brother and sister-in-law believing they should take in your kids because they have a bigger house or more money. Suddenly, your children are caught in the middle of a nasty family feud, all because you didn't draft a Will.

The crux of the biscuit? Your kids might not even get immediate access to any financial assets you intended for them.

Without a clear plan, those funds could be tied up in probate for months, if not years. While the adults squabble over custody and money, your children are left in limbo, uncertain about their future.

What About Your Furry Children?

If you don't make specific plans for your pets, they could face immediate uncertainty about their care and living arrangements upon your death. Without financial provisions, the cost of care might burden whoever takes in your pet. This could deter people from adopting them or limit the quality of care they can provide, affecting your pet's diet, healthcare, and overall well-being.

Moreover, if you own multiple pets, there's no guarantee they will be rehomed together unless specifically stipulated. In cases where no immediate family members or friends can care for the pets, they may end up in animal shelters.

ISSUE TWO:
THERE'S CHAOS, THE FAMILY IS FIGHTING ALREADY, AND YOUR BODY ISN'T EVEN COLD YET.

When you die without any estate planning or without sharing your wishes, your family is left to fend for themselves, which can lead to complete disaster.

Take Sarah's story, for instance. She contacted me after her father died unexpectedly. Sarah lived in Georgia, while her father resided in a neighboring state, closer to Sarah's sister. When their father died, he left no estate plan or documented wishes regarding what to do with his body.

Sarah, believing she knew her father's preferences, began making arrangements with the local funeral home for cremation based on conversations they had over the years. However, her sister remembered differently. She insisted their father never mentioned wanting to be cremated and demanded a traditional burial.

Here's where the real mess began. In the state where their father died, if an individual hasn't formally documented their wishes, the next of kin must agree on the body's disposition. With Sarah and her sister at an impasse, the funeral home had no choice but to place their father in cold storage until a decision could be reached.

This standoff dragged on for four agonizing weeks, filled with emotional turmoil, stress, and conflict. The reality was that Sarah's dad remained in the funeral home until her sister finally relented and agreed to the cremation. The entire ordeal was a nightmare, exacerbating the grief and stress of losing their father.

Without a Will or a prayer, family disputes can turn into epic battles. I always like to say, "Where there's a Will, there's a relative." This means the family starts crawling out of the woodwork when someone dies to see if they were included in the Will. When someone dies without a Will or any estate planning, it's like a scene from the movie *Braveheart*: a fight to the death over who will be in charge, make the decisions, and decide who gets the prized family teapot.

I was once contacted by a woman, Amanda, whose father had died without a Will in the state of Florida. Some states are more lenient than others in terms of probate, but Florida is not one of them. I was schooled on this after attending an estate planning conference where a Florida attorney summarized the probate process in his state by stating, "There are three things you need to know about probate in Florida: Avoid. Avoid. Avoid."

Amanda called me, completely overwhelmed and clueless about where to start. Not only did her father lack a Will, but his adult children had no idea about his financial situation, including a business he owned. Amanda's father had been married five times, was recently divorced, and had a live-in girlfriend who, according to Amanda, had continued using her father's debit and credit cards. Amanda's brother and sister were her half-siblings from a later marriage, and Amanda wasn't very close to them.

Despite repeated attempts to discuss their father's affairs, Amanda received no response, except for a text from her sister stating they had hired an attorney and that Amanda would receive a letter to sign off on them becoming administrators of the estate. Amanda felt hurt, confused, and left out as the oldest sibling; she believed she should be included in the decision-making.

I advised Amanda that you catch more flies with sugar than with vinegar. The best approach might be to appeal to her brother and sister to sit down and have a conversation. They all loved their father and shared a unified goal: to settle their father's affairs according to what they believed he would have wanted.

In these situations, tensions are high, and everyone's patience is tested severely. Before ending the conversation with Amanda, I implored her to consult an attorney herself and also to try to get on the same page as her brother and sister. Otherwise, things were likely to spiral out of control—emotionally, mentally, and financially—very quickly.

FINANCIAL STRAIN ON LOVED ONES AS THEY BECOME A HUMAN ATM

When you die without a Will, your loved ones often find themselves in a financial nightmare because they may not have immediate access to funds to cover final expenses. Unless you've made proactive arrangements like adding an authorized signer to your account, setting up a Payable on Death (POD) or Transferable on Death (TOD) designation on your bank accounts, or having a joint account holder with rights of survivorship, your bank account could be frozen faster than you can say "funeral costs."

Here's how it typically unfolds: when you die, the funeral home files a death certificate, which is tied to your Social Security number. Funeral homes usually notify the Social Security Administration and Medicare of a death on behalf of the family. Once this occurs, any bank accounts linked to the decedent's Social Security number without a beneficiary or joint account holder are frozen.

Even if your account isn't immediately frozen, using a deceased person's bank account or credit card is considered fraudulent. It also complicates the process of distinguishing which expenses were incurred before and after death.

Securing funds for a funeral is no easy task. My uncle died on a Thursday evening, and by Friday afternoon, his bank account was frozen. We thought we had secured a POD or TOD designation on his checking account, but it hadn't been processed correctly. As a result, I had to charge the several thousand dollars needed for his funeral expenses to my credit card.

According to the National Funeral Directors Association, the median cost of a funeral, viewing, and burial in 2024 was $7,848. Cremation is slightly less expensive, with the median cost coming in at $6,970. This is a substantial amount of money for a family to come up with unexpectedly, especially without a Will, as the process of accessing those funds becomes significantly more complicated.

To add insult to injury, a real catch-22 often exists: you need to initiate the probate process to access the funds, but starting the probate process might require paying out of pocket. Without a Will, no one is automatically appointed to be in charge, but to appoint someone, you must go through probate, which requires funds. Thus, your family is trapped in a vicious cycle of needing assets to access assets, creating an endless loop of frustration and financial strain.

I once had a client, Paula, who reached out for help after her uncle's death. Her uncle, a divorced professional gambler without children, owned multiple properties and assets across the US. He was convinced he'd live to 100 and delayed making a Will. Unfortunately, he bet wrong and died at 88. When Paula received a call from the morgue notifying her of her uncle's death, she was caught completely off guard.

Not only did Uncle Ben own several properties, but he also had renters in three of his five properties with active leases. This meant Paula had to quickly ensure that Ben's funeral was paid for but also that a new air conditioning unit was installed in a Georgia property where the HVAC had failed in midsummer.

By the time Paula reached out to me, she had already spent thousands of dollars of her own money on funeral costs, property maintenance, legal fees, and travel expenses to manage his properties. The probate process had just begun, and it would be a long and costly affair before she could be reimbursed.

ISSUE FOUR:

LEGAL LIMBO, DELAYS, AND #PROBATEPROBLEMS

Probate. The word alone can send shivers down the spine of anyone who's tangled with it. The Uniform Probate Code attempts to bring some order to the chaos, aiming to standardize the settling of estates by prioritizing immediate family members like spouses, children, and parents over more distant kin. But even with these guidelines, the reality of probate is often far from streamlined.

What Exactly Is Probate?

Probate is the legal process of administering your estate and transferring your property upon death, either according to the terms of your Will or, in the absence of a Will, under state law. This process isn't just about distributing what you own; it's equally concerned with what you owe. Here's what it typically looks like:

- **Filing the Will and Petition** The process begins with filing the decedent's Will (if one exists) with the probate court to prove its validity. If there's no Will, an application for administration is filed.
- **Appointing the Executor or Administrator** The court appoints an executor (as named in the Will) or an administrator (if there's no Will). This per-

son will manage the estate's affairs.

- **Inventory and Appraisal** The executor must then inventory the decedent's assets and often get them appraised to determine their value.
- **Paying Debts and Taxes** Before any distributions to heirs, the executor pays the estate's debts and taxes from the estate's assets.
- **Distributing the Remaining Assets** Finally, the remaining assets are distributed to the heirs as directed by the Will or, if there is no Will, according to state law.

During this time, the court ensures that estates are settled legally, especially when there is no Will. This means nothing moves—money, property, or otherwise—until the court gives the executor the authority to do so.

And who gets to steer this ship, you might ask? Executors, typically appointed in the Will, can be any trusted and objective individual over the age of eighteen, though they are often family members. If no executor is named, or if the named executor is unable to serve, the role typically falls to the closest relatives, prioritizing the surviving spouse, followed by children and then grandchildren. When multiple individuals are of equal standing, the court may appoint them as co-administrators or choose just one to oversee the entire estate. The executor is responsible for ensuring the fair distribution of assets and the settlement of any debts.

Without disputes, probate can still take anywhere from twelve to eighteen months, depending on the complexity and size of the estate. However with disputes, this process can stretch out for years, filled with bureaucratic starts and stops that can frustrate even the most patient souls.

Consider the story of my client, Selena, whose father died suddenly from a cardiac event. With no estate plan in place, Selena, despite her demanding job, found herself managing her father's affairs. Along with her three siblings, she had to navigate not just their grief but also the immediate financial burdens of their father's funeral, costing over $9,000. Without prior planning, Selena had to front substantial amounts to initiate the probate process and manage creditors, putting her own finances at severe risk.

The burden of probate extends beyond emotional distress; it involves practical financial hardships, too. Imagine maxing out your credit cards just to cover basic probate costs like attorney fees, court costs, and unexpected bills. It's akin to trying to solve a flaming jigsaw puzzle—stressful, painful, and chaotic.

Dying without preemptive estate planning is akin to igniting a fuse on a bomb in the midst of your family's life. The fallout from this explosion affects every facet of your loved ones' lives, from financial ruin to emotional turmoil. It drags your family through a relentless ordeal, battling over your assets while trying to cope with their loss.

Estate planning is not just about directing who gets what; it's about providing clear, compassionate guidance that alleviates burdens during an already challenging time. A little foresight can prevent a colossal disaster, ensuring that your departure from this world is marked by memories of love and respect, not a legacy of legal battles and financial chaos. In the end, a little planning goes a long way in preventing a Grade-A shitstorm dumpster fire from consuming your family when you're gone.

ISSUE FIVE:

WHEN NO PLAN SPELLS A PLAN OF CHAOS FOR YOUR BUSINESS

Owning a business without a succession plan is like driving a car without a steering wheel—eventually, things are going to go off the road. The lack of a clear path forward can lead to operational paralysis or, even worse, internal battles that make Game of Thrones look like child's play.

Imagine you vanish tomorrow—poof! Does your business keep running smoothly, or does it stumble like a toddler in oversized shoes? Without you, will clients still get stellar service? Will employees and vendors still see their checks on time? If you haven't laid the groundwork, you're basically asking your team to sail a ship with no captain, and icebergs are all around.

No succession plan? Brace yourself for the power struggles. Without a designated leader, your business could turn into a wild west of ambitious employees gunning for the top spot. This isn't just about bruised egos; it's about a fragmented vision that could derail the business you've built.

And then there are the legal battles. Without a clear directive, who takes the helm and how your business pie gets sliced can end up in court—expensive, draining, and like watching paint dry. Plus, if your business is a big part of your estate, figuring out its worth and how it's divvied up among your heirs can spark a family feud worthy of a reality TV show.

Prevent this chaos by crafting a succession plan that's as solid as your business foundation. This should include naming a successor and outlining how to control shifts. Don't forget to plan for everyday operations, too, so that the business machine keeps humming, no matter what.

Consider the story of my client, Mira, whose husband, Max, died after a lengthy illness. Max had owned a successful rug business, which was heavily reliant on his personal relationships and industry knowledge. Unfortunately, no succession planning had been put in place, and the business nearly ground to a halt when Max became ill. Mira found herself in a dire situation, with a vast inventory that wasn't selling and a business that was nearly impossible to market to buyers. Without any forward planning, Mira felt her only option was to liquidate the inventory at a fraction of its value—a devastating blow when she needed to maximize returns to secure her financial future.

Get your succession plan in writing, make it official, and share it with all key stakeholders—family, partners, and key employees. It's like providing them with a map in case they need to navigate without you. Ensuring they understand the plan not only secures your business legacy but also protects the livelihoods of those who keep the gears turning.

In short, if your business means the world to you, show it some love with thoughtful planning. A solid succession plan doesn't just secure the future of your business; it acts as a safety net for the people it supports. A bit of foresight now can prevent a major regret later, keeping your business legacy intact and thriving long after you're gone.

A STITCH IN TIME SAVES NINE

It's clear that procrastinating on estate planning doesn't just invite chaos—it practically rolls out the red carpet for it. From leaving your kids in legal limbo to igniting sibling rivalries hotter than a summer barbecue, the risks of neglecting a proper estate plan are too significant to ignore. We've traversed the terrain of financial nightmares and business battles, and the common thread is undeniable: preparation is key.

So, take the reins now. Crafting a comprehensive estate plan might seem like a daunting task today, but it's a gift of peace and stability to your loved ones tomorrow. Remember, in the world of estate planning, a little effort now can prevent a world of hurt later. Let this be the nudge you need to kick-start your journey towards securing a legacy that's as orderly as it is cherished.

CHAPTER 03
TALKING ABOUT IT: WE'RE SCARED TO DEATH TO TALK ABOUT DEATH

The irony of all ironies is that I'm writing a book about death. You see, as a kid, I grew up with an unhealthy fear of death, and the very thought of it scared the bejeezus out of me. I came by it honestly, though. Thanks to my dear old Dad, a small-town doctor, death and sickness were practically additional siblings at our family dinner table. My dad did rounds at the hospital twice daily, so our home phone seemed to ring non-stop with urgent calls from nurses about patients teetering on the edge of death.

Our dinner-time conversations consisted of "Stories from the ER," where my father would regale us with tales of four-wheeler and car accidents, choking incidents, and the myriad of ways everyday folks find themselves flirting with disaster. Our doorstep was no stranger to unexpected visitors, from folks seeking a quick fix for a mysterious rash to one especially memorable afternoon when a desperate parent poured their unresponsive daughter out of their car into our driveway, begging my dad to save her from an overdose of painkillers. She survived and made a full recovery, but it was definitely one for the memory books.

Fifty shades of danger always seemed to be lurking nearby, including another memorable time I nearly took a bullet, thanks to one of my Dad's regulars. Growing up in a small town meant that medical emergencies often led people to call my dad before even thinking of dialing for paramedics. On one beautiful Sunday afternoon, our small-town police department rang up my dad pleading for his help with local yokel Larry, who they knew was a patient of my dad's. Larry was experiencing an especially severe diabetic hypoglycemia episode and was now firing shots into the air in his front yard.

We were too young to be left at home alone, so my dad loaded all three of us into the car, and we headed to Larry's house. Pulling onto his street, it felt like our small, sleepy town had suddenly turned into the south side of Chicago. While the police took cover behind their SWAT-equipped vehicle, my dad pulled into the driveway and ran up to administer a shot of insulin to his patient. I was waiting for a bullet to pierce the glass at any moment, ending my short time on this earth.

The following Thanksgiving, our small town was alerted to two escapees who had fled the local prison and were thought to have been hiding in the woods behind my house. That day, my mom cooked our Thanksgiving turkey with a baster in one pocket of her apron and a pistol in the other. The next day, we noticed our Huffy bikes had been hijacked, so maybe my mom hadn't been overreacting at all.

So, do you see why I grew up as nervous as a sore-tailed cat in a room full of rocking chairs? Surrounded by constant reminders of mortality, I was like a real-life Chicken Little, half-expecting disaster at every turn.

Because of the situational reality of my childhood and my surroundings, I was scared to death of my parents dying. Like unnaturally scared. And then the things I was scared of the most happened—I lost both of my parents too soon.

So my point is, if anyone should be a full-fledged card-carrying death avoider, it should be me. Yet here I am, tackling the taboo head-on with this book. Because, the truth is, skirting around the subject of death doesn't make the Grim Reaper any less likely to knock on your door.

—— ⚰ ——

DENIAL ISN'T JUST A RIVER IN EGYPT

We live in a society that treats death like the forbidden fruit. There's a palpable discomfort around even mentioning the word. We flinch at words like "death," "dying," or "dead," and to maintain our blissful ignorance, we've invented a whole dictionary of euphemisms—passed away, lost, crossed over, bought the farm, kicked the bucket, transitioned—to soften the blow. In fact, a recent poll conducted by Marie Curie, an organization that provides care and support for people with terminal illnesses and their families, has revealed over fifty different euphemisms for death and dying, with phrases I had never even heard of, such as, 'Wearing a wooden onesie," "Coco-pop it" and "Turned turtle." It's almost as if we believe that by talking about death, we're inviting it closer, similar to the old myth that talking about sex will encourage promiscuity among teens. But just as talking about sex won't make you pregnant, talking about death won't make you dead.

This denial is not just a cultural quirk; it profoundly affects our readiness to face the inevitable. We treat death like a lottery we might miraculously avoid. The drive to prepare is smothered by fear and procrastination cocktails. We continuously kick the can down the road, choosing the sweet nectar of denial over strapping on our adulting boots and facing the music head-on.

And trust me, I've floated down that River of Denial myself, especially when my husband and I first decided to draft our Will. Like all good and responsible parents, we decided to get our first Will due to the most asinine reason, which I like to refer to as the "Going Abroad and Don't Want to Orphan Our Kids" panic. A few months after my mother died, my husband and I decided we deserved a much-needed break and distraction and planned an anniversary trip to Mexico. Stirred by the flames of estate nightmares, I was hell-bent on securing our affairs. But that didn't mean that drafting our Will felt like inviting the Grim Reaper to our departure gate. I felt uneasy, superstitious, and on edge. I boarded the plane half-convinced it would nosedive, thanks to our newfound preparedness.

Spoiler alert: I didn't die. Still kicking. Was the experience awkward? Absolutely. But am I relieved we did it? Without a doubt. Was it a blast? Hard no.

Our societal game of peek-a-boo with mortality means that when the inevitable comes, it finds us woefully unprepared, leaving our loved ones to scramble in the dark. This avoidance doesn't cheat death, but it sure does guarantee a bigger mess.

At its heart, estate planning isn't just about who gets grandma's china; it's about safeguarding legacies. Death is the most universal human experience, yet we treat it like an unexpected plot twist. Executors—often our closest kin—are left to cobble together plans amidst their mourning, burdened by our collective reluctance to face reality. So welcome to the club—membership guaranteed, whether you like it or not.

—— ⚰ ——

WHEN PLANNING ISN'T AN OPTION

There are some times when planning ahead just isn't an option. I am well aware that tragedies happen. My dad died at the age of forty-eight, further confirming the fact that life can be brutally cut short. Believe me when I say that I am well aware of the shit that can go sideways.

Not all of us have the resources, time, or knowledge to plan ahead. I get that. This harsh reality hits many of the families I work with, often leaving them in a scramble during already difficult times. Consider the story of my client, Robert, whose world was turned upside down one ordinary evening.

Robert and Eileen were what you'd call late bloomers in love. They settled down after successful, independent careers, keeping their finances and properties separate. Shortly after tying the knot, Robert moved into Eileen's house—still solely in her name, not as joint tenants. The mundane realities of utility and tax bills were all in her name, too. They had begun to sort out their legal affairs, inching towards merging their lives fully, both legally and financially. But life, as it often does, had other plans.

Eileen's sudden collapse and subsequent death at the hospital threw Robert into a whirlwind of grief and urgent responsibilities. When I was brought on board by one of Eileen's closest friends—who also happened to be their financial advisor—I could see the overwhelming confusion mixed with his grief. Robert revealed to me that Eileen had drafted a Will but never signed it. Legally, she died intestate, leaving Robert to navigate the complex process of settling her estate without clear directives.

One of the most heartbreaking aspects for Robert was being locked out of Eileen's digital life. As a nature photographer and a scout for movie locations, Robert cherished the memories they captured together on their travels. But without Eileen's phone passcode, those memories were as distant as Eileen herself. Digital assets, often overlooked in estate planning, can become inaccessible fortresses, sealed off without the right keys.

Robert's situation painfully underscores that you can't just call up Apple to unlock a deceased loved one's phone. Everything you share, every memory stored digitally, can become entangled in bureaucratic red tape if you don't plan ahead. Robert found himself not just mourning Eileen but also battling for access to their shared life, a battle that could have been avoided with a bit of foresight.

TEN OUT OF TEN OF US WILL DIE IN OUR LIFETIME

Statistically speaking, death is pretty much the only certainty we have in life. Yet, when it comes to preparing for it, many of us behave like it's an optional RSVP to a party we never planned to attend. Despite the absolute inevitability of death, most of us put off planning for it like we're trying to set a new world record for procrastination.

Here are the classic excuses I hear all the time, wrapped in denial, dread, or just plain old defiance:

"I'll Be Dead, What Do I Care?"

Take my friend Amanda's aunt and uncle. These two love-birds lived up their retirement in a lavish lake house, surrounded by all sorts of shiny toys like boats and jet skis. When the topic of estate planning came up, their response was a breezy, "Our kids are smart; they'll figure it out." Sure, because nothing says "I love you" like leaving your kids to play a high-stakes game of Treasure Hunt with the IRS and probate courts as spectators. That's not just passing the buck; it's hurling it into a black hole of legal limbo.

"It's Too Depressing to Think About"

Oh, the number of times I've heard this one. It's as if some folks think discussing estate planning is an instant mood killer, like bringing up politics at Thanksgiving. Sure, plan-ning your estate isn't a barrel of laughs, but it beats the pants off leaving your loved ones to play detective with your dusty collection of unmarked keys and mysterious safety deposit boxes.

"I'm Too Young to Worry About That Now"

Recently, during a Zoom call with an aspiring after loss professional, this very topic came up. The woman, a sprightly thirty-four-year-old, seemed to think she had all the time in the world. There she sat, in her cozy home and beautifully decorated living room, telling me she was too young to worry about estate planning. I pointed out, "If you owe or you own, then planning is for you, kiddo."

Death doesn't check your ID. Whether you're thirty-four or eighty-four, if you've got assets, loved ones, or even just your pet fish Bubbles who depends on you, you've got enough reason to start planning.

These excuses are more than just avoidance; they're a direct ticket to complication station for those you leave behind. We're not just talking about an inconvenience. We're talking about transforming profound grief into a logistical nightmare, where mourning takes a backseat to sorting through the chaos you left behind.

In a nutshell, dragging your feet on estate planning doesn't just risk your legacy; it actively gambles with your loved ones' well-being after you're gone. And while none of us can cheat death, we certainly can make our departure less burdensome for those we love. So, let's stop pretending death is optional and start treating estate planning like the absolute necessity it is. Your family will thank you for not leaving them a puzzle with half the pieces missing.

—— ⚰ ——

ESTATE PLANNING—IT'S FOR EVERYONE

The old saying goes, "There are only two certainties in life: death and taxes." Yet, when it comes to estate planning, it seems many treat it as an optional extra—something akin to leather seats in a car you're buying. But here's the real deal: estate planning is not just for the elderly, the wealthy, or families planning for their lineage. It's for anyone who has anything. And by anything, I mean anything from a bank account to a basement full of comic books.

Do you own stuff? Do you owe money? If you answered yes to either, then congratulations, estate planning is indeed for you. It's not just for the silver-haired crowd pondering their legacy over a game of bridge. It's for the young, the old, the single, the married, the divorced, the parents and non-parents, and the pet owners. If you're reading this book, you're the right candidate for estate planning.

From personal experience, I can tell you the process is about as fun as assembling IKEA furniture. Quite literally, no one enjoys planning for their eventual mortality. But let me ask you this: would you rather leave a hot mess for your loved ones to sort through or a well-organized plan that lets them focus on grieving and moving forward? The choice seems pretty clear when you put it that way.

Why It's Important for Everyone

Estate planning isn't about dwelling on death; it's about ensuring control and peace of mind. Here's why it should be on everyone's checklist:

- **Control Over Your Finances** Estate planning allows you to dictate exactly how and to whom your assets—be it your savings account, your car, or your family heirlooms—will be distributed. Without a plan, you're leaving these decisions up to state laws and courts, which might not align with your wishes.

- **Care for Your Loved Ones** It's not just about assets. Estate planning includes making provisions for those who depend on you financially, including minor children. By appointing guardians in your Will, you're choosing who you trust to look after your children, not leaving it up to a court to decide.

- **Avoid Unnecessary Delays and Expenses** Proper estate planning streamlines the process of settling your affairs. It helps avoid the delays and financial burdens that can arise from probate, ensuring your beneficiaries receive their inheritance more quickly and with fewer legal hurdles.

- **Plan for Incapacity** What happens if you become unable to make decisions for yourself due to illness or an accident? Estate planning is critical as it includes creating powers of attorney for both healthcare and finances, allowing you to choose who will make important decisions on your behalf.

- **Peace of Mind** Knowing you have a plan in place that protects your family and your assets can give you immense peace of mind. Think of it as not only planning for the future but also enhancing your quality of life today by reducing anxiety about the unknown.

It's important to remember that estate planning is not a one-time task. As your life changes—maybe you marry, have children, divorce, or your financial situation changes—so should your estate plan. Regular reviews and updates ensure that your plan always reflects your current circumstances and desires.

Estate Planning: Clear as Mud

Let's get real for a moment—the hesitation around estate planning often stems from confusion and hectic lives, not laziness. Estate planning is swamped with jargon and peppered with conflicting advice. Strategies that work for one person may not be ideal for another, and advice from one attorney can starkly contrast with another's recommendations. Often, the fear of navigating this complexity leads to paralysis.

Take the saga with my in-laws—and oh boy, am I really putting my foot in my mouth with this one. While I'm most likely putting my life (and my inheritance) on the line here, I think this is an important story to share.

A few years back, my in-laws decided to update their estate plan, guided by a well-meaning but not-specialized-in-estate-law attorney friend. Their goal was simple: avoid probate. The solution? Add my husband to their property deed and as a joint account holder on their checking account. Easy, right?

However, as we know, the devil is always in the details. Here are a few typical "quick fixes" that often seem appealing to those looking to dodge the formalities of estate planning and probate:

- Scribbling wishes on a piece of paper.
- Verbally telling family members their desires.

- Directly gifting a house to a child or adding their name to the deed.
- Adding a child's name to a bank account.
- Selling a house to a child for just $1.

While these strategies might seem like straightforward solutions, they're more like bandaids on bullet wounds. Yes, you might have saved money on the front end by not paying an attorney for a comprehensive estate plan, and/or they might dodge probate, but with these easy peasy solutions, there could be unintended issues such as:

Legal Validity A scribbled note is hardly a substitute for a Will. State laws have strict criteria for what constitutes a valid Will.

Misunderstandings in Titling Adding a child to a bank account might seem straightforward, but many don't grasp the full implications of what titling really means. This could lead to mismanaged expectations and overlooked tax implications. It's all too common for clients to tell me their parent made one of their siblings a joint account holder, blissfully unaware that this sibling will inherit the entire account. They trust them to "do the right thing"—which, if we're being realistic, could as easily involve a spur-of-the-moment trip to Vegas with the newfound cash, all while completely ignoring potential gift tax implications.

Enforceability of Verbal Wishes As the old saying goes, talk is cheap. Verbal instructions might as well be written in sand at the beach; they're unlikely to hold up legally and can lead to the kind of family disputes that make Thanksgiving dinners awkward.

Tax Complications Transferring property as a gift during one's lifetime, rather than letting it pass through inheritance, might seem like a good idea until you go to sell. For instance, if your parents bought their house for $200,000 and it's now worth $400,000, gifting it to you before their death means you inherit their $200,000 cost basis. Sell that house at its current value, and you're on the hook for capital gains tax on a $200,000 profit—surprise! This can be a hefty financial burden, akin to discovering a termite infestation in the attic.

Loss of Control Adding a co-owner to your property is like getting married; you can no longer make decisions on your own. Every significant choice requires a consensus, and let's just say not everyone's idea of redecorating involves agreeing on paint colors.

Legal and Financial Risks Co-owned property could be endangered if one of the owners faces legal troubles or debt. Creditors might target the property, potentially forcing its sale.

Conflict with Other Estate Plans These strategies might conflict with more comprehensive estate plans, such as a revocable living Trust. For example, transferring a house into my husband's name complicates our ability to manage the estate smoothly, especially if my in-laws' and his deaths were to overlap. Unlikely, yes, but in the world of estate planning, you should plan for every possibility.

Understanding the Full Implications of Estate Planning Choices

This type of scenario underscores why opting for what seems like a straightforward solution can actually complicate matters further. It's essential not to just grab at what appears to be the easiest route but to deeply understand the implications of the estate plan you're considering.

For instance, my in-laws might have benefited from probing their attorney friend about potential downsides to adding my husband to the property deed. By asking, "Are there any potential disadvantages or complications with this approach?" they could have explored the pros and cons more thoroughly. This would have allowed them to make an informed decision and be fully aware of both the benefits and the potential pitfalls.

Consulting with a specialized estate planning attorney is crucial in navigating these decisions. A qualified professional can help you identify and implement strategies that not only meet your immediate objectives but also align with broader financial goals and tax considerations. This approach ensures that the strategies in place are advantageous not just for you but also for your beneficiaries.

Taking the time to understand the full scope of your estate plan, including all potential legal and financial implications, is more than just prudent—it safeguards your intentions and the financial well-being of those you care about. So, before making any significant decisions, it's advisable to seek expert advice to ensure that your estate is managed as smoothly and effectively as possible.

Estate Planning: Simplified and Demystified

The complexity and the heavy jargon often associated with estate planning can be overwhelming, making it tempting to put off or oversimplify crucial decisions. Here are common scenarios where people might stumble, along with straightforward solutions:

- **Procrastination Due to Overchoice**
  Example: Tom is in his 50s and has multiple assets, including retirement accounts, real estate, and a small art collection. He feels overwhelmed by the different strategies and legal options available, leading him to delay taking any action.
  Solution: Start with a simple list. Break down estate planning into manageable steps. Begin by listing assets and liabilities, then consult with an estate planner to prioritize actions. This approach turns an overwhelming task into a series of doable steps.

- **Misunderstanding How Assets Are Titled**
  Example: Linda, a recent widow, assumes that all her husband's assets automatically transfer to her without probate. She is unaware that certain types of assets, like her husband's individually owned stocks, require specific beneficiary designations.
  Solution: Education is key. Estate planning workshops or consultations with an attorney can clarify misconceptions. Linda might benefit from a session focused on how different assets are transferred after death.

- **DIY Estate Planning Pitfalls**
  Example: Kevin uses an online template to create a Will, thinking it's sufficient for his needs. However, his situation, which includes a second marriage and children from a first marriage, is not adequately addressed by a generic plan.
  Solution: While DIY resources are a good starting point for information, hiring an estate planning attorney to tailor a plan can prevent future legal complications and ensure that all personal circumstances are considered.

- **Choosing the Wrong Executor**
  Example: Cheryl chooses her eldest son as the executor without considering his ability to handle the responsibility or his current personal situation, which might not allow him to perform the duties effectively and expediently.
  Solution: Think critically about who is best suited to manage your estate. It doesn't always have to be a family member; sometimes, a professional executor is a better option, especially in complex family dynamics.

By breaking down estate planning into clear, manageable components and addressing common misconceptions, we can demystify the process. The goal is to encourage proactive planning and make the necessary decisions feel less daunting. Remember, effective estate planning is not just for the wealthy; it's a fundamental aspect of managing your legacy and ensuring your loved ones are cared for in the best possible way.

Navigating the Maze with Expert Help

When considering major decisions surrounding your estate plan, always consult with an experienced specialist who can guide you through the potential pitfalls and ensure your actions complement your overall estate strategy, not complicate it. Estate planning might be complex, but with the right help, it doesn't have to be daunting.

Yes, estate planning truly is for everyone. While it's crucial to consult with an experienced estate attorney, being proactive about your own situation is equally important. Always ask questions and strive to understand the implications of each decision. For instance, when presented with solutions, consider asking if there are any cons to this solution to expose any possible pitfalls. Knowledge is power, and the more informed you are, the better you can ensure that the strategies implemented align not only with your goals but also with the best practices for your financial and familial situation.

In summary, discussing and planning for your own death is undoubtedly uncomfortable, but it's essential. It's about ensuring that your loved ones are taken care of and that your legacy is preserved as you wish. Despite the confusion and potential pitfalls, proactive planning is the ultimate act of care, sparing your loved ones from unnecessary stress. After all, good estate planning isn't just for the wealthy; it's for anyone who wants to leave a legacy of love and not a logjam.

CHAPTER 04
ESTATE PLANNING DEMYSTIFIED: WHAT THE HELL IS AN ESTATE PLAN ANYWAY?

So, you're wondering what the hell an estate plan actually is? Well, it's not just a list you scribble on a napkin one night after three too many glasses of Merlot. It's your blueprint for how things should go down after you've left the building—or the planet, to be more precise. Let's break down the not-so-scary building blocks of a robust estate plan without making you yawn or reach for a stiff drink (though, by all means, have one if it helps).

Now, let's clear the air: I'm not a lawyer. I haven't spent sleepless nights in law libraries, nor do I intend to start. My musings here aren't a substitute for bona fide legal counsel. Always, and I mean always, consult with an experienced, seasoned, licensed attorney to navigate the choppy waters of estate law.

My aim is to demystify the scaffolding of estate planning for the everyday person—one average Joe to another. Because it's clear that if crafting an estate plan was as easy as pie, we'd all be bakers. Yet, with nearly three-fourths of Americans floating through life without a Will, it's clear we've got a big problem.

Before we jump into what an estate plan looks like, let's warm up with a few questions you might want to mull over as you read:

- **What's in Your Wallet (and Beyond)?** What kind of assets do you have, and how much might they be worth? Who do you want to inherit these assets, either now or when the time comes?
- **Who's In Charge?** If you're ever out of commission, who do you trust to handle your medical and financial decisions? And who'll take care of any dependents or pets? What about looking after your online life after you've logged off for the last time?
- **Executor and Trustee Picks** Have you thought about who you want to manage your estate or Trust? More importantly, have you checked if they're up for the task?
- **Heartstrings and Heirlooms** Do you have any special items that mean more than money? How do you want those handled?
- **Family and Business Matters** How could your family dynamics influence your estate planning? What's the plan for any business interests you have?
- **The Final Curtain** Finally, what are your wishes for your remains and any ceremonies after you pass?

— ⚰ —

THE MUST-HAVES

WILL

Think of this as your basic instruction manual for the after-life—of your assets, that is. It dictates who gets what, hopefully helping to ensure there's no family brawl over your prized baseball card collection. It's how you tell everyone that your mint-condition Babe Ruth goes to your cousin Jane, not to Crazy Uncle Bob, who is convinced that aliens are after his pension.

The requirements for a legally binding last Will and Testament vary from state to state, depending on where you primarily reside or pay state income tax. Typically, the process is straightforward: you must be mentally competent when you sign your Will, and it needs to be witnessed by at least two individuals who do not stand to benefit from it.

So, what are Some Of the Components of a Will?

Testator's Info That's you, the star of this document. At the core of a Will is the testator—the person who drafts the document to specify how their assets should be distributed and who should care for any dependents.

Declaration of Intent Just a way of saying, "Yes, I want this to be my Will."

Executor Appointment The ringmaster who'll ensure your circus runs smoothly after you've left the tent. We'll talk about this more later in Chapter 8, but be sure the person you choose is selected after careful thought and consideration. Make sure this person has the tools to do the job, the time and temperament, and a heads-up that they've been pegged.

Beneficiary Designations This part outlines who gets everything from your sock collection to your stock options. However, it's crucial to understand that Wills do not override beneficiary designations on things like retirement accounts and life insurance policies. These assets will pass directly to the named beneficiaries, regardless of what your Will says. So, while drafting your Will, remember to review and update beneficiary designations on such accounts to ensure they align with your current wishes.

Guardianship Appointments If your cast of characters includes minors, appoint a guardian to step into your shoes. This ensures they're in good hands if the unthinkable happens.

Signatures and Witnesses Your autograph is needed to seal the deal, witnessed by at least two people who aren't in the inheritance line-up. Their signatures verify that they observed you signing the document and affirming it as your Will.

Drafting a Will is like scripting your final act because, without it, you leave the stage open for interpretative chaos and run the risk of potentially pitting loved ones against each other in a battle royale over who gets the last laugh—and the family heirlooms.

TRUST

There's a common myth that Trusts are reserved for the ultra-rich—think mansion owners and private jet flyers. But in reality, whether you live in a studio apartment or a sprawling estate, setting up a Trust can be a wise strategy for anyone looking to safeguard their assets for loved ones.

Despite their benefits, many people don't fully grasp what a Trust is. Imagine a Trust as a treasure chest, but not just any chest—it's a legally savvy one that safely holds your assets, like money, property, and stocks, until it's time to hand them over.

Understanding the Basics

A Trust is essentially a legal document where you, the grantor, set terms for how your assets are managed and eventually passed on to your beneficiaries. The person at the wheel of this operation is the trustee, and they've got the all-important job of making sure your assets do what you want them to do when you're not around to oversee them. Here's how it works:

> **The Setup** You, as the grantor, are the person who decides to set up this Trust. It's like saying, "Hey, I've got these treasures, and I need a safe place to keep them until the right time."

> **The Keeper** Enter the trustee. This person (or sometimes a company) is like the trusted captain of your ship. They make sure your treasure chest is well-kept and that everything inside is managed according to your map— err, your Trust documents.

The Beneficiaries These are the folks or charities you've chosen to receive your treasure when the time is right. They may not get to snatch up the treasure right away; they have to wait until certain conditions are met, like reaching a certain age or maybe when you're no longer around to manage it yourself.

Types of Trusts

You've got two main categories: revocable and irrevocable.

Revocable Living Trusts: Your Estate's Flex Pass

This type of Trust is popular because it's adaptable—you can make changes as your life and circumstances evolve. It's active during your lifetime, and you get to see your estate plans in action. You can tweak it, add assets, or completely overhaul it without much fuss. Plus, when the curtain closes on your life's play, this Trust hardens into an irrevocable Trust, locking in your wishes exactly as you set them.

Now, let's dispel a major myth: Keep in mind that a revocable Trust won't shield your assets from debts and creditors. Also, having a Trust does not mean you can forgo a Will. You still need what's often called a pour-over Will, which acts as a safety net to catch any assets that might have slipped through the cracks and ensures they make it into the Trust posthumously.

Irrevocable Trusts: Locking It In

While revocable Trusts offer flexibility, irrevocable Trusts are all about commitment. Once you create an irrevocable Trust and move assets into it, there are no take-backs. You're essentially locking those assets away, relinquishing control to ensure specific benefits that a revocable Trust can't provide. The main appeal of an irrevocable Trust is its power to protect. Since you no longer own the assets you transfer into the Trust, they're generally protected from both creditors and estate taxes. This kind of Trust is a fortress, safeguarding your assets from claims and, often, hefty tax bites.

Why Use a Trust?

It's not just about keeping things tidy. One of the most popular goals of a Trust is its ability to avoid the probate process, which can save both time and money. Unlike a Will, which only kicks in after you die and usually requires court approval, a Trust can take effect before death, after death, or if you become incapacitated.

Trusts can serve a variety of purposes. They can help transfer property smoothly, minimize estate taxes, ensure privacy, protect assets for minors until they come of age, and make sure your wishes are carried out exactly how you'd like, especially if you're not around to oversee things.

In essence, setting up a Trust is a way to ensure that your assets are taken care of without the interference of probate court, making the transition smoother and sometimes quicker for everyone involved.

Several years ago, amidst the chaos of launching my business and life ramping up, my husband and I realized that our estate plan was more like a rickety old jalopy we'd snagged off Craigslist—functional, sure, but liable to conk out at any moment. Recognizing the need for a robust upgrade, we consulted a seasoned trust and estate attorney, someone adept at navigating the complex needs of busy families. After some discussion, we opted to incorporate a revocable living Trust into our estate strategy.

The day we were set to sign our revamped estate documents, I had a eureka moment, courtesy of a painful encounter with a Lego brick left by my kids' continued inability to clean up after themselves. It struck me then how much Legos resembled the assets and debts in an estate. Typically, when someone dies, dealing with their estate can feel like a frantic scavenger hunt for Legos—under the couch, in the bathtub, across the bedroom floor. Without a clear plan, these pieces can be scattered far and wide, leaving a monumental task for the executor.

But with a Trust, it's as though you're preemptively gathering all those Legos into a designated box. This proactive organization means that rather than roaming a proverbial minefield of assets, your executor simply retrieves a "well-labeled box," neatly packed with everything in its right place. Think of a Trust as this box—a tool that organizes your assets efficiently, ensuring they're directed exactly where they should go without any fuss. Isn't that a relief?

Expertise Required

Not all attorneys are experienced Trust wizards and know how to create one properly. I've seen it firsthand. Remember the advice that my in-laws once got from their attorney friend? They were told that you only need a Trust if you're swimming in a Scrooge McDuck pool of money—$5 million or more. That's just not right. I've consulted with many attorneys who have cautioned that there's no real line in the sand for when to establish a Trust. The reality is that the decision to establish a Trust should consider multiple factors such as your age, family dynamics, future earnings potential, your goals, and more—not just your current net worth. If your lawyer provides a cookie-cutter answer, probe deeper. This is your legacy, after all; ensure the advice you receive is tailored to your specific needs and goals.

Why Trusts Rock (When Done Right)

Setting up a Trust might be pricier than a simple Will, but think of it like investing in a top-notch mattress. You're paying for comfort and peace of mind. It's about making sure your estate skips the probate pitfall and keeps your affairs out of the public eye.

Funding the Trust

Here's where many drop the ball. A Trust only works its magic if it's properly funded—that means actually transferring your assets into it. Without this crucial step, your Trust is like a car without gas: pretty but stationary.

Take the tale of my client, Morgan. After her mother died, she helped her father overhaul his estate plan, setting up a revocable living Trust and a pour-over Will with Morgan as trustee. The plan was brilliant—but quite literally, only on paper. It was supposed to shield them from probate and ensure immediate access to funds after her father's death. The hiccup? After Morgan's father died and she hired me to help her as the trustee and executor, we found out that none of his assets—nope, not even the family home—had been titled to the Trust. Unfortunately, the Trust was, in essence, empty, which meant that Morgan would have to go through the probate process. This was the exact scenario the Trust was supposed to prevent. And there I was, breaking the bad news that all the time and money invested hadn't secured the smooth transition they'd hoped for.

So, while Trusts might not be the solution for every single estate planning challenge, they offer a robust way to manage your legacy—ensuring it's handled just the way you want, without the drama.

FINANCIAL POWER OF ATTORNEY

A Financial Power of Attorney (POA) is essentially your financial bodyguard. It empowers someone you trust implicitly to manage your finances—not when you're overindulging but when you're seriously incapacitated. This lets someone you really trust handle your money if you're out of commission—think coma, not just a hangover.

Key Misconception

One big misconception is that a power of attorney is still applicable after someone dies. However, it punches out the same moment you do. Yes, dead. So, it's a living document for the... well, living.

This document isn't just about ensuring the electricity bill gets paid on time; it's a crucial line of defense against scams targeting those who might be vulnerable, like an elderly relative who's a prime target for a scammer who wants to go on a Walmart gift card shopping spree.

Moreover, the POA allows your chosen agent to step in and manage your affairs seamlessly if a sudden health crisis leaves you unable to make decisions or communicate. This can range from paying daily bills to handling complex financial negotiations.

In the unfortunate event that you become incapacitated without a POA in place, your loved ones may have to go through a guardianship process to gain legal authority over your affairs. Guardianship is a court-appointed role where someone is legally tasked with the care and decision-making for another adult who is deemed unable to manage their own care or finances. This process can be lengthy, emotionally taxing, and costly.

A Real-Life Scenario

Let me share the story of my client, Nora, which underscores the critical importance of comprehensive estate planning, particularly a Financial Power of Attorney (POA). Nora faced an unforeseen crisis when her husband, Nathan, suffered a massive stroke in his mid-forties, rendering him unable to speak, write, or manage any communications. Despite his excellent rehabilitation care, Nathan was incapable of discussing or managing their finances.

Nathan had always been the financial guru of the family, meticulously managing their investments, bills, and multiple bank accounts, including some in his name only due to his Canadian citizenship. Just a week before his stroke, he had taken steps to ensure Nora was informed about their financial situation by sharing a detailed financial spreadsheet with her. Tragically, the sudden nature of his illness meant that Nora was left in the dark; she knew the spreadsheet existed but couldn't access it because she couldn't recall the password to Nathan's laptop.

Nora and Nathan had been in the process of organizing their estate, including setting up a financial POA, but they hadn't finalized it. When Nathan became incapacitated, Nora found herself legally locked out of his personal accounts—even though they were married and had some joint accounts, Nathan had managed most of their finances independently, and only he knew the passwords to many of their accounts.

Recognizing the complexity of their situation, the attorney assisting Nora with guardianship proceedings referred her to me specifically to aid in the discovery process of finding online financial accounts. This was a complex and emotionally taxing process that could have been mitigated if the POA had been finalized. My role was to help Nora try and navigate the digital and financial labyrinth left in the wake of Nathan's incapacitation, ensuring she could access critical financial resources during this crisis.

Nora's story highlights the importance of proactive financial planning. A properly executed POA would have allowed Nora to manage the family's finances without interruption, avoiding additional stress during an already devastating time. Her experience serves as a crucial lesson: estate planning is vital not only in the event of death but also in instances of sudden incapacitation. It's about ensuring continuity and security, safeguarding not just physical assets but also maintaining the operational side of life's necessities.

MUST-HAVE:
ADVANCE DIRECTIVES FOR HEALTHCARE

Navigating the unexpected requires planning, especially when it comes to healthcare. Advance directives are vital documents that articulate your preferences in medical situations where you might not be able to communicate your decisions. These directives typically encompass the following:

Living Will This document specifies your wishes regarding medical treatment in scenarios where you cannot communicate your decisions yourself. It outlines what you want if you're knocking on death's door—whether you're all in for every life-saving contraption or prefer to skip the drama and go gently. It's essential to understand what signing this document means. Contrary to popular myth, having a living Will doesn't mean doctors will rush to "pull the plug" if you're in an accident. These directives come into play only under specific circumstances, such as when you cannot advocate for yourself or when all viable treatment options that could lead to recovery have been exhausted. It's not a Disney Fast Pass to the end; it's a well-considered plan for your most vulnerable moments.

Durable Power of Attorney for Healthcare Separate from the financial power of attorney, this specifically covers decisions about medical care when you're incapacitated. This person is your voice when you can't speak. Choose wisely; this person decides between what you'd actually want and what might seem like a good idea after watching *Grey's Anatomy*.

Here's why these directives matter: I was fresh out of college, had just started a new job, and was attending my first professional conference in Washington, DC. I was drifting off into a peaceful sleep when my cell phone rang. It was from a nurse at the hospital where my grandmother had been admitted. They couldn't locate her advance directives, and with her condition worsening, they needed to make immediate decisions.

I'll never forget what she said to me: "Your grandmother is close to coding, and we need to know whether or not to resuscitate her. I really don't want to crack a nintey-three-year-old's rib cage with the defibrillator if I don't need to."

Fortunately, I was familiar with my grandmother's wishes—she had explicitly expressed her preference against resuscitation. This allowed me to convey her wishes confidently, sparing her the invasive procedures she had hoped to avoid.

It's vital to make informed decisions about your healthcare directives. Many people misunderstand these documents, thinking that they are giving up control over their treatment by signing them. Remember, these directives are not about hastening your end but about safeguarding your rights and dignity if you're unable to make decisions yourself. They ensure that your medical care aligns with your wishes during times when you might not be able to express them.

MUST-HAVE:
LONG-TERM CARE PLANNING

Decide early whether aging in place or moving to a spot like Shady Pines (complete with bingo and margarita Mondays) is in your cards. Plan now to enjoy later.

Think about where you might want to live as you age and how you want to be cared for. This isn't just practical; it's crucial for ensuring comfort and quality of life later on.

MUST-HAVE:
FINAL ARRANGEMENTS

Instructions for your funeral, burial, or cremation. Do you want a traditional burial? An ash scattering party in Cabo San Lucas, complete with a craft tequila tasting? Your life's last bash can be anything you want; just make sure your loved ones know what this is and that it's written down somewhere. This can be part of your Will or a separate document, but it is crucial to ensure your wishes are respected.

MUST-HAVE:
IMMEDIATE ACCESS TO FUNDS

There are various methods to ensure immediate access to funds after your death, but it's crucial to consult an experienced estate attorney to find the best option for your specific situation. A common approach is to add someone as a joint account holder with rights of survivorship, which allows the surviving owner(s) to inherit the funds directly upon the death of another owner. This method grants full access to the account at any time.

Alternatively, you can appoint someone as an authorized signer on your account or use Payable on Death (POD) or Transfer on Death (TOD) designations. These strategies allow your designated beneficiaries to access the funds directly without undergoing probate while maintaining control over the account during your lifetime. Each of these options facilitates immediate access to funds, ensuring a smoother transition and less bureaucratic hassle for your loved ones.

MUST-HAVE:
UP-TO-DATE NAMED BENEFICIARIES

Ensuring your beneficiary designations are up to date is one of the most crucial steps in estate planning, in my opinion. These designations are powerful tools that allow assets such as retirement accounts, life insurance policies, and even some types of bank accounts to bypass the probate process entirely and pass directly to the individuals you've specified. Think of it as giving VIP passes to your heirs, letting them skip the long lines of legal limbo. But here's a tip: Mark your calendar to review your beneficiary designations annually and update them as needed to ensure the right people inherit your assets without any mix-ups.

MUST-HAVE:
LIST OF ASSETS AND LIABILITIES

No one likes surprises, especially the kind that involve hidden debts or unknown assets popping up like unwelcome plot twists. Keep a clear, up-to-date list of what you own and what you owe. This transparency helps your loved ones handle your estate with precision, avoiding potential financial landmines that could disrupt their grief process.

MUST-HAVE:

BUSINESS SUCCESSION PLAN

For business owners, it's vital to outline a clear succession plan. This strategy should detail how your business will be handled or transitioned in the event of your death or incapacitation, ensuring its longevity and continued success.

MUST-HAVE:

DIGITAL ASSET INVENTORY

As our lives become increasingly digital—from social media profiles to cryptocurrencies—these assets also demand thoughtful planning. Begin by ensuring your executor knows all the accounts you possess to prevent them from slipping into obscurity or the wrong hands.

Crafting a plan for who will manage your digital presence, covering everything from social media to online banking, will ensure these assets are properly handled. While creating a comprehensive digital asset inventory might be tedious, it's an indispensable component of modern estate planning. Assign a trusted individual to oversee these digital assets, providing them with explicit instructions on how they should manage or distribute them.

MUST-HAVE:

ACCESS INFORMATION

Don't forget the practical details like the passcode to your phone or the password to your computer. Make sure a trusted individual knows how to access these crucial points of entry. However, if you have young children or grandchildren, there's a good chance they already know these details as a result of moments you've handed over your device for a bit of quiet during dinner at a restaurant. This familiarity can be a double-edged sword; it's convenient but underscores the need for thoughtful management of who knows your access information.

———— ❢ ————

NICE-TO-HAVES

NICE-TO-HAVE:
LETTERS OF INSTRUCTION

This document may not be legally binding, but it is pure gold for guiding your loved ones. Think of them as the cheat sheet for your life's finale. In my legacy organization work, I help clients draft these not just as documents but as roadmaps for the family treasure hunt—sans the old map and "X marks the spot." These letters outline personal wishes and key facts, serving as a behind-the-scenes director's cut of your estate plan.

NICE-TO-HAVE:
PROPERTY INVENTORY

Ever heard the one about the family feud over Grandma's cookie jar? Not funny. That's why a comprehensive inventory of your personal property—yes, even those kitschy salt-and-pepper shakers—is crucial. It's not just about economic value; it's also about sentimental stakes. Detailing who gets what can keep peace in the family and ensures that your vintage comic book collection goes to the niece who'll treasure it, not just eBay it.

NICE-TO-HAVE:

PLANNING FOR YOUR PETS IN YOUR ESTATE

Clearly, Fluffy isn't going to trot down to the bank and cash a check. So making provisions for your furry family members is your way of saying, "Someone will feed you, and yes, they'll buy the good kibble." In your estate plan, you can make arrangements for your pets either in your Will or pet Trust. While you can appoint a guardian for your pet in your Will and allocate funds for their care, keep in mind that these funds are treated as a gift and can be used at the guardian's discretion. Thus, it's crucial to choose someone trustworthy. Furthermore, provisions made in a Will only take effect after probate, which can delay the availability of funds for your pet's care.

Alternatively, a pet Trust provides a more secure and immediate way to care for your pets after your death. In a pet Trust, you appoint a trustee to manage the funds and a caregiver to look after your pet. You appoint a trustee to manage the cash and a caregiver to handle the cuddles. This setup isn't just for the rich and furry; it ensures Fido's funds are used strictly for his spa days and squirrel patrols, bypassing the slow-moving probate process. Trust us, Rufus will thank you in more ways than just tail wags.

NICE-TO-HAVE:

GUARDIANSHIP INSTRUCTIONS

Choosing a guardian for your kids is like casting the lead in a play where you won't see the performance. These instructions don't name the guardians—they will be outlined in your Will. Instead, they detail your wishes for your child's upbringing, including their education, religion, financial support, and whatever else you'd like to include. This document reflects your trust and hopes, serving as a record of how you want your child cared for if you're not there to run the show. It's your crucial advice to ensure that the reins are held by someone who truly understands your parenting aspirations.

NICE-TO-HAVE:

ORGAN DONATIONS AND BODY BEQUESTS

Bummer alert: Parkinson's Disease runs in my family. So when my uncle was diagnosed in his late fifties, he registered as a donor to the University of Miami Brain Endowment Bank. By donating his brain after death, he could give researchers the ability to answer important questions about what goes wrong when a disease affects the brain and, hopefully, help change the trajectory for others.

Fortunately, my uncle shared these wishes with me so that we could make arrangements to facilitate the donation when the time came. The day of my uncle's death, even before he had died, I called the Brain Endowment Bank's 24-hour hotline to start getting the wheels in motion. He had been the longest active donor on their list, so it was meaningful to be part of bringing this plan to fruition.

Ideally, they like to harvest the brain within eight hours, and the brain donation must take place within twenty-four hours of a person's death. After a couple of hours of trying, it was clear that the donation wasn't going to be easy. I was getting desperate, and unfortunately, after almost twenty-four hours of trying, we were unable to find a pathologist in his hometown of Rochester, NY, to perform the brain harvest. I was heartbroken. This had been the one final wish I'd hoped to fulfill for my uncle and for me as well because this might have direct consequences for my health. I had no idea this would be a possible obstacle. However, I quickly learned that even though almost 170 million people are registered to be donors, only three in 1,000 people die in a way that allows for deceased organ donation.

Bottom line: if you want to donate your organs or leave your body to science, make these wishes known in your plan and also include specifics of the actual donation to make sure this goes without a hitch. Consider even doing a dry run if the donation is going to be more complicated, such as finding a pathologist to actually harvest the organ.

BRINGING DOWN THE CURTAIN ON YOUR ESTATE PLANNING SHOW

Did you find that listicle as thrilling as watching paint dry? If I'm nodding off just writing it, I can only imagine your struggle. But much like convincing kids that broccoli is a superhero food, I'm here to spell out the essential—albeit less exciting—steps to safeguarding your future.

Now, after you've meticulously checked off every item from your estate planning list, the next move is to bring your inner circle into the loop. This isn't just about handing over a stack of papers; it's about orchestrating a clear plan of action. Gather your family, executor, and any key players, and lay out the game plan. Think of it as a strategic family game night where the stakes are much higher than Monopoly money.

Estate planning is not a "set it and forget it" kind of deal. It's an evolving process that demands regular updates as your life changes and laws evolve. By staying on top of this, you ensure that your final adieu is as seamless and stress-free as possible—not just for you but for everyone you hold dear. Consider this your ultimate parting gift: a meticulously organized exit strategy.

An estate plan is more than just a collection of documents. It's a carefully crafted roadmap that guides your loved ones through the complexities of what you've left behind, ensuring that your final curtain call is as smooth as a French Sancerre, minus the legal hangovers. With a little foresight and a lot of organization, you can help prevent a family circus that rivals any reality TV show. So, line up your ducks—or teapots—and rest easy. By taking care of the nitty-gritty now, you'll spare your family from becoming the stars of their own dramatic saga, battling over who gets the silver spoons.

Remember, a bit of planning today helps keep the family feuds at bay. Secure your legacy, and perhaps, you'll find peace knowing that your farewell won't be the spark that ignites the next big family uproar.

CHAPTER 05
IGNORANCE ISN'T BLISS: WHAT YOU DON'T KNOW WON'T KILL YOU, BECAUSE YOU'LL ALREADY BE DEAD

The phone rings. On the other end, a voice crackles through, heavy with the weight of fresh loss. "I don't know where to start," they confess, adrift in the sea of estate settlement. You might think these calls come from those left behind by someone who never bothered to create a Will. But nope, you'd be dead wrong. Ironically, the vast majority of these callers are not clueless heirs but named executors, armed with a Will and supposedly ready to navigate the aftermath.

So what's the rub? you might wonder.

Well, let me tell you, it's a doozy.

When my mom died, I couldn't differentiate a Power of Attorney from a Power Ranger. In other words, I was clueless about the necessary documents, the required actions, and, most importantly, the first steps to take. To compound the issue, I suddenly found myself responsible for an aging loved one who was in cognitive decline and facing significant health issues.

Unfortunately, this scenario is all too common. Often, losing a loved one means taking on the care of someone left behind—be it a surviving spouse, an aging parent, or a dependent child.

Despite having their ducks seemingly lined up—Will drafted, healthcare directives, powers of attorney all set—many find themselves blindsided. The heart of the problem? A document-centric approach to estate planning rather than a strategic one. Folks often sit down with their attorney, whip up the necessary paperwork, and prance out the door without a second thought, blissfully unaware that they've just set the stage for potential chaos.

Now, don't get me wrong, I'm not necessarily placing the blame on anyone in particular here—not the attorney or the folks doing the estate planning. It's just that most people would rather not linger on the topic of estate planning any longer than necessary. Why would we spend any more time on unpleasant activities than we have to? Would you spend extra visits at the gastroenterologist's office?

Heck, if it were possible, I bet most people would bundle in the perfunctory estate planning tasks along with their drive-thru meal just so they could get it out of the way: "I'll take a Big Mac, large fry, diet coke, and throw in a simple Will and Testament, please... oh and a colonoscopy too."

What they fail to grasp is how critical it is to mesh their estate plan with their life's broader objectives and nuances.

They overlook crucial aspects that don't fit neatly into standard documents.

The result is a plethora of blind spots that no one could have warned them about because, frankly, most people don't see them coming. As we've covered, people don't spend a lot of time planning for death. And just to be clear, this isn't about pointing fingers or assigning blame. It's simply the harsh reality many face when they discover that having a Will isn't the magic bullet they hoped for.

—— ⚰ ——

INACCESSIBLE FUNDS

Navigating the financial aftermath of a loved one's departure can often feel like trying to solve a Rubik's Cube in the dark. Surviving loved ones are thrust into a frantic scavenger hunt for funds desperately needed to cover immediate and often hefty expenses. As we peeled back the curtain earlier in Chapter 2, the lack of swift access to funds isn't just an inconvenience—it's a gaping hole in both non-existent and many estate plans alike.

The Cost of Saying Goodbye The financial impact of a death in the family can be staggering. Consider this: I was once contacted by a family reeling from the sudden loss of a loved one. To add insult to injury, they were confronted with the staggering reality of a $30,000 funeral bill. It's an enormous burden at a time of profound grief. According to the 2023 General Price List Survey Report by the National Funeral Directors Association (NFDA), the average cost of laying someone to rest was $8,300. When you factor in a burial vault, which is often necessary, the total can jump to $9,995. These numbers aren't just sobering; they're downright daunting.

Ensuring Access to Funds When the decedent is the family's primary breadwinner, or they hold accounts solely in their name, the surviving family members' access to these funds can be severely delayed. The processing of a death certificate can sometimes take weeks and, in rare cases, even months, especially in extraordinary circumstances like those experienced during COVID. During such crises, delays of three to four months were not uncommon, leaving families financially in limbo for months.

Titling and Beneficiary Designations It's crucial to confirm that all financial accounts are correctly titled and that beneficiary designations are up to date. This ensures that funds are accessible to the spouse or other beneficiaries without unnecessary delays. Without proper titling, significant assets can get tied up in legal processes, which are unavailable to those who need them most.

Adding Signers vs. Joint Account Holders As individuals age, they often consider adding an adult child or loved one to their bank accounts to assist with paying bills. However, this well-intentioned plan can lead to unintended tax implications. By adding an adult child as a joint account holder, you're effectively making a gift of half the account's balance, which could be subject to gift tax implications. Instead, consider adding them as signers—not co-owners. They get access without the tax headache. It's like having their cake and eating it too, without having to cut off a piece of funfetti for Uncle Sam.

Strategic Planning for Immediate Needs

When it comes to handling finances after a loved one dies, navigating the maze of red tape can feel like you're stumbling through an obstacle course blindfolded. But don't worry; there are some strategic maneuvers you can pull off now with the help of a trust and estate attorney or financial advisor to ensure your loved ones aren't left figuring out the money maze when they should be mourning.

Here's a couple of options:

Purchase Life Insurance Numerous attorneys I collaborate with recommend life insurance as an optimal solution for covering immediate after loss expenses. This preference is due to life insurance policies typically being among the first to disburse funds. By designating a beneficiary, they receive the death benefit promptly after the insurance claim is processed and approved, ensuring swift access to necessary funds following the insured's death.

Set Up a "Final Expenses" Account Like a VIP pass, this account can bypass the usual probate hold-ups, giving your family immediate access to the funds needed for immediate expenses after you're gone.

Consider POD and TOD Accounts Think of a Payable on Death (POD) account or a Transfer on Death (TOD) designation on investment accounts like a baton pass in a relay race—smooth and direct. These ensure that certain assets transfer directly to a named beneficiary without getting tangled up in probate. However, it's important to remember that these designations override instructions in Wills or Trusts. If a POD or TOD account is set up to benefit one person, it can lead to unequal distributions

among heirs despite any equalization provisions specified in other estate documents. This setup ensures quick
access to funds but may not reflect a broader intent for
asset distribution among all children or beneficiaries.

Joint Accounts with Survivorship Rights It's like a co-pi-
lot on your financial journey. If one goes, the other automatically takes over without a hitch. Just keep in mind
that you should discuss possible tax implications with
your attorney or financial advisor.

Prepay Your Exit From buying your burial plot to prepay-
ing funeral home services, locking these down can lift
a heavy burden off your family's shoulders. But here's a
thought—what if the funeral home goes out of business,
or what if you change your mind? That traditional burial
with a walnut casket and silk pillow you selected might
evolve into a preference for a more eco-friendly green
funeral down the road.

Research Burial Insurance Often called final expense or
pre-need insurance, this can be a straightforward way to
earmark funds for your send-off. According to Consumer
Reports, premiums might run you $50 to $100 monthly
for a $10,000 death benefit. But be warned, the numbers
game might not always be in your favor. Over time, you
could end up paying more in premiums than the actual
payout, a point highlighted by the Funeral Consumers
Alliance (FCA).

By putting these strategies into play now, you're not just planning for the inevitable; you're giving your loved ones the gift
of peace—they can focus on healing without the financial
headache. Think of it as setting up the game board in their

favor so when the time comes, they're ready to play without scrambling for pieces.

———— ♦ ————

NOT KNOWING ASSETS AND DEBTS

One of the most common requests I seem to have these days is, "Can you help me find my loved one's accounts?" It's no surprise, really. Paper statements have gone the way of the dodo, making it challenging to trace your deceased loved one's financial footprint. This common conundrum is not only a result of most accounts being online with statements delivered electronically instead of via mail, but it also leaves families completely in the dark about whether they've gathered all of the assets and liabilities of the decedent.

The Executor's Treasure Hunt

One of the first—and arguably most daunting—tasks for an executor is to compile a comprehensive list of assets, debts, and liabilities. It sounds straightforward enough until you're knee-deep in paperwork, discovering that your loved one's financial life is as complex and layered as a triple-decker novel.

I once had a client, James, whose father died at the age of 104. He lived a wonderful life—never sick or in the hospital a day in his life—and died peacefully in his sleep. When James called me to ask for my help, I extended my condolences, to which James replied, "Don't be sorry. My dad lived a long, beautiful life and was fortunate enough to die peacefully in his sleep. I hope to be that lucky."

Deciphering Decades of Data

James's father might have won at longevity, but he left behind a historical saga of financial documents, some dating back to the 1940s. James sent me packets of papers to sift through—documents that chronicled a lifetime of financial activities. While his father had been meticulous in preserving every piece of paper, it turned out that most of these accounts had long been closed, transferred, or liquidated. The archival avalanche made our treasure hunt more like an archaeological dig—excavating relics that no longer held value but needed to be sifted through nonetheless.

The Hidden Pitfalls of Unknown Liabilities

And let's talk about the flip side—liabilities. Not knowing about any open lines of credit or outstanding debts can turn an already challenging situation into a full-blown crisis. Will the house be foreclosed? Is the car about to be repossessed? Are there tax liens lurking around the corner, ready to jump out like financial bogeymen? This side of the blind spot can leave executors not just frustrated but genuinely fearful of what might pop up next.

I once had a client, Mary, whose husband, Victor, died after a short illness. In the wake of his sudden departure, Mary uncovered a jarring financial reality: Victor had left behind several credit cards, all maxed out, with one carrying a staggering balance of over $40,000. As a general rule, if your spouse dies you are not personally responsible for their individual debts unless it's a joint debt or state laws make you liable. However, despite not being a co-signer on the credit card, Victor's estate was responsible for settling this debt. This situation starkly illustrates a critical point: debts do not disappear with the debtor.

Mastering Your Estate's Financial Landscape

To prevent this from becoming a burdensome ordeal for your loved ones, here's a proactive approach to managing your estate effectively:

Compile a Comprehensive Asset Inventory

Start by cataloging everything you own—no item is too small if it holds value:

> **Real Estate and Vehicles** List properties and vehicles along with their market value.
>
> **Valuable Personal Items** Include jewelry, artwork, collectibles, and other high-value items.
>
> **Financial Accounts** Gather recent statements from your bank accounts, investment portfolios, and retirement plans.
>
> **Secure Locations** Document the contents and locations of safety deposit boxes and home safes.
>
> **Insurance Policies** Detail each policy, including life, health, and property insurance, noting cash values and death benefits.

Assess and List All Liabilities

Understanding your financial obligations is equally important:

> **Debts** Record all liabilities, including mortgages, loans, credit lines, and any other personal debts.
>
> **Ongoing Expenses** Note any recurring payments that may impact the estate, such as property taxes or utility bills.

Update and Verify

> **Annual Review** Make it a habit to update this inventory annually or after any significant life event or purchase.
>
> **Name Changes and Mergers** Keep track of any changes

in institution names or account statuses, especially for older accounts that might have undergone transformations or mergers.

Assess Business Assets

If you own a business, replicate this inventory process for all business-related assets:

> **Business Valuation** Include an up-to-date valuation of your business.
> **Company Assets and Debts** List all company-owned assets and outstanding debts.
> **Operational Accounts** Document all operational accounts and key business agreements.

Implementing This Plan

By maintaining a detailed and current inventory of your assets and liabilities, you provide your executor with a clear roadmap. This reduces the guesswork and potential for oversight, ensuring a smoother transition and administration of your estate. Moreover, it guards against the loss of assets due to outdated information and ensures all debts are accounted for, preventing surprises for your heirs.

Staying organized with your financial information isn't just about making life easier for those you leave behind—it's about ensuring your legacy is handled according to your wishes with the least amount of stress possible. Keeping a detailed and updated inventory is a straightforward step that pays dividends in clarity and peace of mind for everyone involved.

ACCESS TO OR AWARENESS OF DIGITAL ASSETS

When my grandmother died, I remember going to her metal, avocado-green file cabinet, where everything was cataloged and neatly organized—paper bills, account statements, receipts, every single tax return since 1942—each piece of paper was neatly organized in file folders and labeled in my grandmother's meticulous cursive handwriting. I can still smell the hint of must and mildew.

Well, welcome to the 21st century, where storage solutions float in the cloud, and the keys to our kingdom are password protected—passwords that you're probably forgetting even as I type this.

Death is final, but your digital life lingers like the last guest at a party. Today, we're entangled in a sprawling digital web that spans social media accounts, online banking, digital photo albums, and a plethora of subscriptions—each as crucial to your legacy as those dusty knickknacks were to Grandma.

While your digital assets are very much a part of your assets and debts, as outlined in the second biggest blind spot I encounter, many people don't even think to include them as part of their asset and debt inventory.

Defining Digital Assets: So, what's a digital asset anyway? There is really no agreed-upon definition of what a digital asset is, but in the book *Digital Asset Entanglement: Unraveling the Intersection of Estate Laws & Technology*, digital assets "include electronic communications, financial records (but not necessarily the underlying asset), documents, information, videos, and pictures stored on devices, platforms, or clouds or maintained or managed online."

Imagine everything you've ever posted, purchased, or stored online. Your tweets? Digital assets. Your cloud-stored vacation snaps? Digital assets. Your frequent flyer miles? Yep, those are digital assets too.

Here's a quick rundown of what can be lurking as your digital assets, which comprises your digital estate:

- **Online Accounts** Your virtual self's home.
- **Digital Photos & Videos** Where memories reside in pixels.
- **Social Media** Every "like" you've ever made.
- **Emails & Instant Messages** Digital chitchat that never dies.
- **Cloud Storage** Your personal slice of the data cloud.
- **Health Records** More revealing than your diary.
- **Subscriptions** From Netflix binges to Amazon shopping sprees.
- **Cryptocurrencies & NFTs** Digital gold mines.
- **Domain Names & Blogs** Your slice of the internet real estate.
- **E-commerce Profiles** Your shopping personalities.

These assets can hold different types of value, including:

- **Monetary** Need I say more?
- **Sentimental** Those heart-tugging vacation videos.
- **Exchange** All those frequent flyer miles.

Executor's Digital Dilemma When the inevitable happens, it's up to an executor to make sense of this digital maze. But here's a staggering fact: less than one-third of American adults have a Will, and even fewer have thought about their digital afterlives.

And let's not even start on the outdated lists of usernames and passwords—some haven't seen an update since we were all taking the Ice Bucket Challenge. As an executor as well as an after loss professional, I've seen too many digital assets dissolve into black holes.

Why does it matter? Because unclaimed digital assets mean potentially lost money for heirs. Unpaid bills can accumulate because nobody knows the online account exists. Ongoing subscriptions can continue siphoning funds from the estate. And all those digital accounts floating around unchecked can lead to breaches of privacy and security.

Privacy After Death: A Survey Insight And let's not forget privacy: a recent NetChoice-Commissioned survey found that 70% of Americans want their digital communications to remain just that—private, even after death. About 43% hope these communications are deleted outright, while only a brave 20% are okay with their executor peeking into their digital lives, but only if they had previously given consent.

Legal Labyrinths and Emotional Webs However, it's important to remember that digital privacy can be a double-edged sword. A case in point involved Mike, a successful attorney in his forties whose sudden death left his family grappling with a digital quagmire. Mike had a Will, but like many, it hadn't been updated to give his executor access to not only tangible assets but to digital assets as well. His family did not know the unlock code for his phone or the passwords for his computer or email accounts. Consequently, his online life—

bank accounts, social media, cloud storage—was locked away, as inaccessible as a safe without a combination.

The challenge with digital assets isn't just the technological barrier; it's the legal and procedural morass you sink into when trying to access them posthumously. For instance, Apple and Google, stewards of much of our digital lives, have stringent protocols to guard against unauthorized access. Furthermore, many of the terms of service that accompany these custodians' tools or platforms specifically disallow third-party access, regardless of the relationship.

When Mike's family sought to unlock his accounts, they were met with a process more complex than they anticipated. Apple required a court order to even consider granting access to Mike's data, a process that would pile legal fees on top of grief. Meanwhile, Google had shut the door on us because Mike's brothers, in their desperation, had made multiple failed attempts to guess his password, triggering protocols that locked his account permanently, even from his legally appointed executor.

This client experience underscores a crucial gap in modern estate planning: the digital realm. Many don't realize that digital assets need to be explicitly included in estate plans. Without clear legal authority to access or administer digital assets, companies are obligated to protect the privacy of their users or the terms of service, even in death. This leaves families not just grieving but utterly perplexed by the barriers between them and their loved ones' online legacies.

So, what can you do to prevent this digital conundrum?

Step 1: Create A Digital Asset Inventory

Think of this like gathering all your digital ducks in a row. Start by listing everything in a digital format that has value—from your Gmail account to your Instagram, from your PayPal to your crypto wallets. You can use a digital vault, a basic spreadsheet, or even go old school with pen and paper. The critical step is to maintain this list meticulously—update it whenever you add new digital assets or change existing information. Additionally, ensure that the right person knows how to access this inventory.

Create and secure a list of the following:

- **Device unlock codes**, including those for older devices
- **Email accounts**, including older or less frequently used ones
- **Social media profiles**, including any inactive accounts
- **Financial accounts**, including online banking, payment services such as PayPal, investment portfolios, and brokerage accounts
- **Cryptocurrencies** like Bitcoin, non-fungible tokens (NFTs) and digital artwork
- **Digital content** such as eBooks, music files, and photo libraries
- **Online accounts** across various platforms, especially those with subscription services
- **Reward programs**, including airline miles and other loyalty points
- **Cloud storage services**, detailing where digital files or photos are stored
- **Intellectual property**, including digital patents, trademarks, and copyrights
- **Business assets**, including domains, logos, and creative content

As you catalog these, consider pruning the digital dead-wood—accounts you no longer need or use. This not only simplifies your digital estate but also secures it. And with tech giants moving towards passwordless logins, now's the perfect time to ensure your access methods are future-proof.

Step 2: Utilize Available Online Planning Tools
These tools are like the secret agents of your digital estate, working undercover to ensure everything transitions smoothly if you're not around to log in. Many platforms now offer ways to appoint someone to manage your accounts posthumously without sharing your password collection.

Here's a quick toolkit rundown:

- **Facebook's Memorialization Settings** Ensure your Facebook presence is handled the way you want after you've logged off for the last time.
- **Apple's Legacy Contact Feature** It lets you designate someone to access your iCloud data when you're no longer able to.
- **Google's Inactive Account Manager** Google can notify your trusted contact if your account goes inactive for a set period, allowing them to manage parts of your digital legacy.

Step 3: Keep Your Info Correct, Complete, and Current
It's not just about having digital assets but knowing where they are and how to access them. This means keeping a detailed record of everything from login information for your online accounts to access codes for more critical data like financial records and cryptocurrency. Consider jotting down a simple note or creating a digital document outlining where to find this info and how to use it. Think of it as leaving breadcrumbs for your loved ones to follow in the digital forest. Consider

using a digital vault that complies with current encryption standards. For instance, the one I use is 256-bit encrypted and password-protected.

As you're storing and documenting current information, please remember that sharing passwords might feel harmless—it's actually against most terms of service agreements. Also, keep in mind that many companies are shifting towards passkeys, which allow users to authenticate and log in without having to enter a username or password.

For better security:

- Use multi-factor authentication (MFA) or two-factor authentication (2FA) whenever possible.
- Opt for long, unique passwords—think 18-26 characters.
- Avoid leaving passwords on Post-it notes or a sheet of paper around your desk.
- Use a cloud-based or locally stored password manager.

A password manager can be your digital sidekick here, helping you generate and store strong passwords and keep your online life organized. It's also a handy tool for updating your inventory of accounts and making it easier to delete ones you no longer need.

Here are the 6 Best Password Managers according to Forbes, with what they felt was best about each one:

- **NordPass** Best browser extension with passkey generation
- **Dashlane** Best password customizations and password health tool (also, this is what I use personally)

- **Bitwarden** Best affordable open-source solution
- **1Password** Best password manager for beginners
- **KeePass** Best free password manager
- **Keeper** Best multifactor authentication customization

Step 4: Chat With Your Attorney
Now's the time to ensure your estate plan is up to snuff, especially regarding digital assets.

Here's your checklist for the attorney visit:

- Confirm your estate documents are in line with state laws concerning digital assets.
- Ensure your power of attorney includes permission for your agent to access digital assets, especially if you become incapacitated—think mortgage payments or urgent bills.
- Check that your executor has authority over both your tangible and digital assets.
- Ask your attorney to stay updated on the best practices for managing digital assets as the digital world evolves rapidly.

This discussion with your attorney will help protect not only your physical assets but also the digital legacy you'll leave behind. Making these conversations part of your regular estate planning check-ins can save your family a lot of headaches later.

Wrapping up on Digital Assets: As we navigate the complexities of our increasingly digital lives, it's crucial to ensure your digital legacy is as carefully planned and protected as your physical one. By taking proactive steps today, you can safeguard your digital assets and ease the burden on your loved ones, making your digital farewell as orderly as your physical goodbye. This attention to detail ensures that your digital footprints lead not to confusion but to cherished memories and well-managed legacies.

Before we move on, please note that if you own a business, creating a digital asset inventory is crucial to ensure business as usual for your hard-earned business.

—— 🪦 ——

A POTPOURRI OF OTHER BLIND SPOTS

No Overarching Strategy

Without a comprehensive plan, even the best legal documents can fall short. Most people treat estate planning like a quick coffee run—order at the window, grab your drink, and you're on your way. They meet with an attorney, rattle off what they think they need, and walk out with a Will, maybe a Trust, and a few other documents.

But here lies the obstacle: what's often missing is a comprehensive strategy. Sure, a Will can specify who inherits your vintage guitar or your secret stash of rare coins, but it doesn't address the broader nuances of a well-rounded estate plan.

Estate planning shouldn't just be about distributing assets; it's about crafting a plan that aligns with your overall life goals, values, and the specific needs of your heirs. Without this strategic layer, even the most detailed legal documents can fall short, potentially leaving your loved ones mired in complications that could have been avoided with a little extra planning foresight.

The Great Document Hunt: Locating Essential Papers

One of the most common hurdles in administering an estate is not knowing where to find crucial documents like Wills, Trusts, insurance policies, and lists of assets and liabilities. Finding these documents should not be akin to an Easter egg hunt because this oversight can delay proceedings and add layers of complexity and frustration for your executors and beneficiaries.

Ensuring that all important documents are not only well-organized but also easily accessible is a simple yet overlooked necessity in estate planning. I can't tell you the number of clients who come to me after losing a loved one and say, "I think my [fill in the blank] had a Will, but we can't find it. I think the Will might be in the safe deposit box, but I'm not sure."

Yes, locking your Will in a safe deposit box shows foresight, but forgetting to tell anyone where the key is? Not so much. It's like hiding the treasure map but forgetting you've made an actual map.

After my mom died, I started going through her house. As I sifted through her possessions, I stumbled upon a bewildering collection of keys. She had mentioned having a safe deposit box, but which key belonged to it—or if there were multiple boxes—was anyone's guess. Each key was a mystery: was it for a safe deposit box, the old shed out back, or perhaps, a portal to Narnia? This absurd situation left us not just with physical clutter but a puzzle that could have been easily avoided with a bit of preemptive organization and clear communication.

Lack of Executor Preparation

We must acknowledge that appointing an executor is often treated like a game of Pin the Tail on the Donkey—blindfolded and haphazard with hopeful, yet misguided, stabs in the dark. The truth is, most people spend more time deciding who gets the antique spoon collection than on preparing the executor on how to wrangle estate duties effectively.

Consider the case of my client Richard, who was named executor by his Aunt Joan. Aunt Joan lived in the South, far from Richard, who was on the other side of the country. Despite his role, Richard was not informed about any aspect of her financial situation. When Aunt Joan passed away, Richard was left to piece together her estate with little more than a pile of disorganized documents—some of which referenced assets that were no longer valid or had not been properly managed after the death of her husband. This lack of preparation led to months of additional stress and delay, complicating the distribution process to other heirs.

Many assume that being an executor is as simple as following a recipe. Yet, without guidance, they could be cooking up a disaster worthy of a kitchen nightmare episode. Arm them with knowledge, not just documents, unless you want your estate handled like a mystery box challenge on Chopped.

Complex Family Dynamics

Imagine your family as a series of intricate gears in a watch; each turn affects the others, often in ways you didn't expect. A Will might divvy up the assets cleanly, but it won't necessarily prevent the gears from grinding or snapping. That's because documents don't deal with Sunday dinner snubs or the undercurrents of long-held grudges.

Focusing solely on legal documents while ignoring the soap opera of family dynamics is akin to bringing a knife to a gunfight—it's underprepared and overly optimistic. A strategic approach might involve setting up family meetings mediated by a professional or even some preemptive therapy sessions to ensure that the transfer of assets doesn't spiral into a "Family Feud" episode.

Estate planning can be especially tricky for blended families, where dynamics involve children from both current and previous relationships.

Consider the case of Kylie, who came to me through her attorney, desperate for assistance in unraveling her father's complicated estate. Despite her father's sudden death, he had reassured Kylie that everything was in order, including a Trust and a Will, placing her as a beneficiary poised to inherit a part of his legacy. However, the situation swiftly became murky when Kylie's stepmother became evasive about the estate details immediately following his death, claiming no Will existed.

Typically, alongside a Trust, a pour-over Will is crafted to catch any assets that may not have been properly titled to the Trust, addressing any oversights or recent acquisitions. Yet, Kylie's stepmother insisted there was no Will, leading to all marital assets defaulting to her as the surviving spouse. Feeling sidelined and suspect, Kylie, acting on the information given, applied for and was appointed as the administrator of her father's estate.

Haunted by her father's assurance of a Will, Kylie faced a stonewall from her stepmother, who now controlled the narrative—and potentially, the assets. Despite the lack of proof of any foul play, Kylie was determined to pursue her father's assets as his only direct descendant.

Kylie's predicament highlights a critical point: while you can't always thwart deception, one can't help but wonder if thorough planning with an experienced estate professional might have safeguarded her father's intent to provide for his only child. Effective planning, clear communication, and consideration of all family dynamics are crucial in preventing such ordeals, ensuring that your estate plan executes exactly as you wish while minimizing potential conflicts.

Unmarried Partners

These days, more folks are choosing to live together without tying the knot. According to the U.S. Census Bureau, as of 2023, living together without being married is 40% more common than it was twenty years ago. But here's the kicker: even with these shifts, if you're not married, you're often skating on thin legal ice when it comes to rights and protections that married couples take for granted.

Let me be clear: I'm not here to judge anyone's lifestyle choices about cohabitation. But, it's critical to acknowledge that unmarried couples often lack the legal protections that married couples have. It's an unfortunate reality, and ignoring it doesn't help anyone.

Take my client Leah, who had recently lost her partner Carter. They were together for a solid fifteen years, and they raised Leah's now-grown kids from a previous marriage. Scarred by her first divorce, Leah was more than okay with not walking down the aisle for the time being. Carter was her person, and that was enough—until it wasn't.

Carter owned the house they lived in, and his name was the only one on the deed and mortgage. Leah pitched in on the payments, sure, but on paper, she didn't have a stake. They thought they had things sorted with Carter's Will naming Leah as executor, figuring she'd manage his affairs and keep living in the home they shared.

Well, when Carter passed away, all hell broke loose. His sister stepped in, challenged the Will, and suddenly Leah found herself on the outside looking in. She wasn't even able to say goodbye at his funeral, which his sister arranged without her, in another state. And as if that wasn't enough, with Carter's accounts frozen amid the legal back-and-forth, the mortgage payments stopped. The bank didn't want to hear Leah's side of the story because her name wasn't on the mortgage. Before she knew it, the house was foreclosed, and Leah had to pack up fifteen years of life and memories.

The bottom line is that if you're in a committed relationship but not married, it's crucial to have a formal estate plan to ensure your partner can manage your affairs or inherit your assets. Unlike marriage, there's no automatic legal right for partners to act on each other's behalf or inherit assets. You must explicitly grant these rights through a valid estate plan.

Updates and Maintenance

Treating your estate plan like a "set it and forget it" crock-pot is a recipe for disaster. Life isn't static—your estate plan shouldn't be either. Changes in laws, financial status, or personal relationships can turn yesterday's perfect plan into today's bewildering maze. Think of your estate plan as software that needs regular updates to avoid bugs. Without these periodic tune-ups, you might as well be navigating with an outdated map, leading your heirs straight into a bureaucratic quagmire. And no one likes being stuck in the mud, especially when they're already dealing with loss.

The American Bar Association Commission on Law and Aging recommends revisiting your advance directives based on the "5 D's" to ensure they remain appropriate and effective, but I think this can be general advice for reviewing your entire estate plan as well. These pivotal life moments include the death of a loved one, a divorce, receiving a new medical diagnosis, a significant decline in health, or entering a new decade of life. These events can significantly alter your circumstances, making it crucial to review and potentially revise your estate plans to reflect your current needs and wishes.

Misaligned Real Estate Titling and Unintended Beneficiaries

The devil, as they say, is in the details, and these details often come with their own set of pitchforks after a loved one's departure. Take, for example, the story of my client, Emily. After her husband lost a courageous battle with cancer, Emily found herself entangled in a mesh of paperwork that seemed to contradict the very purpose of their meticulously drafted estate plan. They had managed to sidestep the formal probate process since most of their assets were jointly owned or designated directly to her.

Their primary residence was titled in joint tenancy with rights of survivorship, seemingly securing her immediate ownership. However, the waters muddied when it came to their cherished lake house, discovered to be solely in her late husband's name. Contrary to their belief and planning, this oversight thrust Emily into the throes of probate, incurring unexpected costs and delays—a stark reminder of the necessity of ensuring asset titles reflect the intentions of the estate plan.

Another common oversight is the beneficiary designations on life insurance policies. Imagine the disbelief when a client finds that the life insurance proceeds they thought were meant to secure their financial future instead land in the lap of an ex-spouse. This isn't just an awkward oversight; it's a financial faux pas that can rival some of the best (or worst) plot twists in soap operas.

Such a scenario unfolded when a client discovered that his father's life insurance payout had been sent to an ex-wife, all because the beneficiary designations were never updated post-divorce. This misstep turned what should have been a straightforward financial provision into a prolonged legal skirmish, underscoring the importance of regularly reviewing and updating all beneficiary designations to ensure they align with current intentions and life circumstances.

To avoid such pitfalls, it's imperative to set up assets with proper titling from the outset. This involves not only reviewing titles and designations regularly but also consulting with a trust and estate attorney who can navigate the complex interplay of laws that might affect how assets should be structured. For instance, considering whether assets should be held in trust, as joint tenancies, or under other forms of ownership can prevent many of these issues. A solid estate plan is more than just a document; it's a dynamic strategy that adapts to changing life circumstances and laws, ensuring that when the time comes, your wishes are executed as smoothly as possible without burdening your loved ones with additional grief.

Ensuring Seamless Estate Execution

It's crucial for everyone involved—not just the person crafting the estate plan—to grasp the details of how each component functions. This understanding guards against misinterpretations and ensures that the estate is administered smoothly, truly honoring the decedent's wishes. More than just a bureaucratic necessity, this clarity can significantly reduce stress during an already challenging time of grief.

Consider your estate plan as a master blueprint. If every piece is clear and every instruction detailed, you minimize the risk of disputes and confusion. This proactive approach does more than simplify legal processes; it preserves peace and harmony among those you love when you're no longer there to mediate.

By thoroughly addressing these elements now, you're not merely planning for the inevitable; you're actively safeguarding your legacy from becoming a tangled affair that burdens your family. Instead of leaving behind a saga that could unravel at the family gatherings, ensure that your legacy supports the celebrations of life that follow—where the conversations are about memories and joy, not conflicts over assets.

So, take the reins firmly in your hands. Plan meticulously, update regularly, and communicate clearly. Let's keep family reunions focused on the sweet moments—like sharing a slice of pie—not piecing together a puzzle you've left behind. In doing so, you ensure that your farewell is just as orderly and harmonious as the life you lived.

CHAPTER 06
THE STUFFADEMIC: NOBODY WANTS YOUR HUMMEL FIGURINE COLLECTION

I like to say my mother was a high-class hoarder. She had a penchant for collecting—not just any items, but antiques, period pieces, antiquities, and pretty much anything random and expensive that caught her eye. Once my siblings and I were grown and flown, our childhood home became her blank canvas, and her obsession with themes led her to deck out entire rooms to reflect specific historical or cultural motifs.

My mother's fascination reached its peak when she became obsessed with Shaker-style furniture and fixtures after tracing our family lineage back to descendants of the Shakers. If you know anything about the Shaker religious movement, you'd know that anyone who chose to become a Shaker made a conscious decision to join a celibate, communal religious sect. So, the fact that I'm a descendant suggests that someone was doing more than shaking their bible. This intriguing, slightly scandalous heritage sparked her obsession with

Shaker furniture and artifacts, leading her to transform her living room into a full-blown Shaker extravaganza. I jokingly started calling her a Shakaholic.

But her thematic adventures didn't stop there. Each of our childhood bedrooms was transformed according to a different theme—one in Native American decor, another in Scottish flair, and one entirely devoted to her sewing passion. It was extraordinary.

While these themed rooms—complete with matching furniture, knickknacks, artwork, and supplies—brought her immense joy, they made my blood pressure soar every time I visited home.

To compound the issue, in her retirement years, she started working at Scott Antique Market, aka the World's Largest Monthly Indoor Antique Show. This was like leading a fly to a rib roast and only fueled her obsession further. It was akin to a chocoholic working at the Hershey's factory. On one occasion, she came home with a 19th-century cricket cage. When I asked why on earth she had acquired such a thing, she simply said, "Well, I didn't have one, Rachel!" And really, you can't argue with that.

But, let me tell you, for something so tiny, that cricket cage became a massive presence in my mind. The damn cricket cage became the emblem of all the items I'd one day need to sort through. While these things tickled the heck out of my mother and made her happy, they only left me with dread.

The week after my mom died, I went home to check on the house. The fridge was still full of food, her car was parked in the driveway, and the mail was spilling out of the mailbox.

But what really made my blood boil? That damn cricket cage. What was I supposed to do with it, along with the thousands of other items my mother had amassed over the years? I distinctly remember sitting on the floor and breaking into tears. The irony of it all is that I was surrounded by so much stuff but had never felt so empty.

But this is a tale as old as time because brace yourselves, ladies and gentlemen, for the Great Stuffademic—a deluge of possessions accumulated by our beloved Baby Boomers and the Greatest Generation. They've gathered more treasures and trinkets than any thrift store could manage.

⚰

THE ROOTS OF THE STUFFADEMIC

OK, before we go any further, I need to say something in defense of my mom, as well as the Greatest Generation and all the Boomers. It's important to note that, in my view, they aren't entirely to blame. My mother often recited the popular saying coined by Calvin Coolidge, stating, "Use it up, wear it out, make it do, or do without" as a nod to being raised by veterans of the Great Depression, they learned to see every door knob and knickknack as a future heirloom or a ticket to potential riches. These aren't just items; they're badges of a lifetime's labor and thrift, a tangible LinkedIn profile of their material achievements.

However, this "more is more" philosophy is on a collision course with the "less is more" approach of Millennials and Gen Z. These youngsters often see experiences as the new status symbols, not the overstuffed curio cabinets or the garages-turned-warehouses that might give Marie Kondo a nervous breakdown.

For Boomers, parting with their treasures can feel like deleting chapters of their autobiography. Every garage sale item or donated vase isn't just decluttering; it's an existential crisis packed in bubble wrap.

Consider the story of Brenda, a client who came to me after the death of her mother. Brenda had been the primary caregiver during her final years. After her mother died, Brenda found herself paralyzed, unable to decide what to do with her mother's belongings. As her mother had also believed, Brenda thought these items held intrinsic value and should be preserved for future generations.

Rather than sorting through her mother's belongings immediately after her death, Brenda moved everything into a storage unit—on top of the myriad of boxes already filling her garage from when her father died and her mother had moved into a senior living facility. Now, she was paying hundreds of dollars a month to store these items, bleeding her finances without any return on investment.

Nine months later, Brenda reached out to me to help manage the daunting task of unloading the contents of both the storage unit and her garage. This situation presented a significant challenge: she was continuing to pour money into storing items that were unlikely to yield any return. In fact, it would cost her more to pay my team and me to attempt to sell or donate these items—many of which had been crammed into a cramped space and significantly damaged during the move. The once desirable mid-century modern furniture, now scratched and marred, had lost much of its value and appeal.

When I visited the storage unit, my heart sank. The damage was worse than expected, and it was clear that most of the furniture would be difficult, if not impossible, to sell. At this point, the harsh reality set in: the costs of storing, sorting, and attempting to sell these items were simply compounding her losses.

This scenario is all too common among Baby Boomers and their heirs. The emotional attachment to belongings, coupled with the financial strain of maintaining them, creates a complex dilemma. It highlights the need for a strategic approach to handling possessions before they become burdensome.

As older generations downsize, their Millennial and Gen Z heirs often look on in mute horror. The thought of integrating a forest's worth of mahogany furniture into a minimalist, plant-filled apartment is about as appealing as a root canal. It's not just a storage issue—it's a clash of cultures, values, and aesthetics.

——— ⚰ ———

PACK YOUR BAGS: WE'RE GOING ON A GUILT TRIP

Up until a few years back, my family was the custodian of a home in Eastern Tennessee, passed down since 1890. This wasn't just any house; it was where my great-grandparents had settled, where my grandmother first saw the light of day, and where my mother grew up. It was a turn-of-the-century Victorian beauty crammed to the rafters with every conceivable memento of our family's past. From delicate china and gleaming silverware to crystal, knickknacks, old handwritten letters, faded newspaper clippings, quirky coin collections, and, yes, a massive collection of big, brown furniture—it was all there.

This family home was not just a building; it was a tapestry of history, set in Harriman, Tennessee, a town famously dubbed the "Utopia of Temperance." In this planned community, alcohol was the ultimate forbidden fruit—any hint of it threatened property confiscation. If those walls could talk, the tales they'd tell! The items in that house weren't just objects; they were the chapters of our family's story, each with its own voice in our heritage.

After my mother's death, the decision to sell this treasure trove of Victorian splendor was agonizing. Yet, the toughest challenge was figuring out what to do with all the contents.

Growing up, my sister and I were indoctrinated with the belief that these treasures, especially the bulky brown furniture, would one day adorn our own homes. My mother, bless her heart, had us swear to preserve these "priceless" relics as if they were sacred. They were, in her eyes, the tangible essence of our heritage to be forever cherished. We swallowed the narrative hook, line, and sinker, setting off on what felt like a never-ending guilt trip, navigating the sentimental landscapes of our family legacy and clinging to a promise made to our departed mother.

Fast forward, and my sister's and my homes became orphanages for the big brown furniture and knickknacks that our mother passed down. One day, almost simultaneously, my sister and I'd had enough. Guilt be darned—we were fed up. No disrespect to Mama, but this was ridiculous. We decided it was time to find new homes for these pieces, places where they would be appreciated rather than serve as burdensome artifacts of obligation.

So, what if, instead of dumping our cluttered past on our heirs, we chose a different route? What if we crafted a plan that allowed for a nostalgic journey without the baggage of guilt?

This is a dilemma I encounter far too often these days. I once worked with Ellie, a client who lost both parents in her early twenties. Struggling with the demands of starting a business, motherhood, and executor duties, Ellie was particularly stumped by her mother's spoon collection—those collectible spoons from different states. It was clear: those spoons were more than just collectibles; they symbolized her mother. Yet, Ellie was stuck, unable to decide their fate, paralyzed by the weight of the memories they held.

This scenario is all too common. We inherit not just possessions but the emotional narratives tied to them. It's crucial to recognize that while these items carry memories, letting them go doesn't erase those memories. They are, after all, just things: spoons, furniture, knickknacks. Remembering this can be the first step towards moving forward, unburdened, and ready to create our own stories.

And while we're at it, let's delve into the saga of family photos. During the cleanout of our Tennessee house, I unearthed literally thousands of photos, their ages ranging from the late 1800s right up to the flashy 1980s. And thanks to the era of Wolf Camera and its penchant for double prints, my archival challenges doubled. Remember the trip my grandparents took to Banff in 1974? I found two prints of every single scenic shot. That flowery bush my grandmother adored? Yep, got two shots of that beauty, too.

Sorting through mountains of photos, I realized I didn't recognize half the faces staring back at me. It dawned on me just how vital it is to manage these snapshots of the past effectively.

Here's my two cents: organize your photos meticulously. Label them clearly. If you have duplicates, keep the best and recycle the rest. Consider digitizing the keepers to preserve them for future generations. Instead of arranging them by year—which can be tedious and less straightforward—try sorting them by holidays, significant events (like graduations or school plays), or even by the people featured. This way, you not only save space but also make these memories more accessible and meaningful to everyone who might one day take a stroll down memory lane.

— ⚰ —

WAIT, WAIT, DON'T TELL ME YOU WANT THAT PIE PLATE?!?

Okay, I know I'm about to sound contradictory, but hear me out. While many family members genuinely don't desire heaps of inherited stuff, there's a catch—they might not want it unless they see someone else eyeing it or if it's something that reminds them of their loved one but has no value. In my experience, the fiercest disputes revolve around items with negligible monetary value but immense sentimental significance.

Family squabbles over inheritance usually bring to mind images of siblings bickering over bank accounts or real estate, but it's the sentimental tokens—like mom's quirky teapot or dad's old fishing hat—that ignite the fiercest fires, particularly in blended families. Ironically, the very items that might not fetch a dime on eBay are the ones that could cost your family its harmony.

Here's the kicker: even though everyone may turn their noses up at your Hummel figurine collection, let someone else show interest, and suddenly it's as precious as the Crown Jewels. It's human nature—nobody wants your stuff unless they see someone else holding it. Suddenly, it's a free-for-all, with "Well, she got more than I did" accusations flying. Cue the family drama.

Many well-meaning folks think a vague clause in their Will—something like, "Let my heirs divvy up my personal items as they see fit"—will prevent World War III. Spoiler alert: it doesn't. Instead, it's like handing them a grenade with the pin already pulled. A more bulletproof strategy? Specify who gets what. Yes, down to that kitschy Elvis Presley snow globe. Then, have a family sit-down to explain your choices.

Transparency might not cure all jealousies, but it can certainly prevent a few.

—— 🛑 ——

IF YOU AIN'T FIRST, YOU'RE LAST

The immortal words of Ricky Bobby from the movie *Talladega Nights* ring surprisingly true in estates. As I said before, it's often not about the bulky furniture or outdated china, but rather the items that carry sentimental value, like Grandma's pie plate or potential cash value like a gold coin collection that can easily be grabbed. Sadly, it's usually a race—whoever pulls up first claims the prize.

Here's the hard truth: when a home stands empty, it can turn into a free-for-all. Maybe it's the cousin claiming rights to grandma's jewels for her chauffeur duties or the uncle who eyes the antique silverware. Suddenly, everyone's racing to claim their share.

I once had a client managing an estate embroiled in years of litigation. One major conflict arose when, shortly after the family matriarch died, a relative dashed to the house and absconded with a multi-million dollar coin collection hidden in a closet. I'll never understand why such a valuable collection was stowed in such a manner, but that's beyond my judgment.

While some family members are just outright thieves, some family members often feel their actions are justified, claiming, "Well, I took Mom to the doctor every day for three years—I deserve her diamond watch!" And so the justifications spiral.

Take, for instance, my client, Judy, who lived in a different state from where her brother and aging mother were living.

After her mother died, she discovered that her mother's jewelry collection had vanished. Upon arriving at her mother's house and checking the place where the jewelry had been stored, she was stunned to find all the jewelry boxes empty. Sadly, Judy knew her brother had taken it all and most likely sold it. However, Judy felt her hands were tied. If she accused her brother of this crime, an epic brawl would break out, and their already strained relationship would further deteriorate.

First things first? Lock it down. Whether it's a house, car, or boat, securing the property is crucial. You wouldn't believe how many "friendly neighbors" suddenly want to browse through belongings after someone dies—yes, it's as creepy as it sounds.

Furthermore, these tales are all too common and highlight the need for clear, specific directives in estate planning to prevent misinterpretation and opportunistic behavior in the wake of a loss.

—— ⚰ ——

IS THIS A PRICELESS VAN GOGH OR A KNOCKOFF FROM HOMEGOODS?

Handling an estate isn't just about dividing assets; it's also about understanding what those assets truly are. Many executors face the daunting task of deciphering the value, provenance, and details of various items, often under challenging circumstances.

For example, my uncle bequeathed his extensive collection of tubas to several beneficiaries, including local music organizations. The problem? I'm no tuba expert. Differentiating between a rare vintage piece and a standard model was beyond my ken, making the distribution a complex puzzle.

Then there was David, a client whose mother had left behind what she claimed was a rare and valuable art collection. She had name-dropped artists like Dr. Seuss and Salvador Dalí, so expectations were high. I called in an art expert from Atlanta to assess the collection. Unfortunately, her initial excitement evaporated upon closer inspection. What was touted as original pieces turned out to be mass-produced, signed, and numbered prints—commonly sold as "serigraphs" on cruise ships.

In David's case, he was misled about the collection's worth—a not uncommon scenario where executors are left to navigate a maze of misinformation.

But there's another side to this coin. If you possess genuinely valuable items, ensure you provide detailed appraisal and authenticity documents to your executor. We've all heard those urban legends—like discovering a Rembrandt in the attic or finding a Renoir at a yard sale because the family assumed it was a cheap reproduction. Just as it's heartbreaking to learn your treasured painting is worth diddly squat, it's even worse to discard something that could potentially bring a significant windfall to the estate. While discovering a hidden masterpiece is rare, it's not impossible. Ensuring your executor has all the necessary information can prevent such costly oversights.

CAUGHT BETWEEN A SWORD AND A HARD PLACE

In the years leading up to my uncle's death, as his cognitive abilities continued to decline due to Parkinson's disease, thankfully, he didn't seem to lose his sense of humor or his memory of his inside jokes. For years, he talked about his "navy swords" in a locked closet, and for years, I didn't give it a second thought. My uncle was in the Navy, and I remember thinking, "Did they even have swords in the Navy…?" I thought it was either something I didn't know about or that he was really starting to decline cognitively.

Well, one day, I found out exactly what he meant by "Navy Swords," which had absolutely nothing to do with alleged military paraphilia.

As his care needs increased, we decided it was time to move him into an assisted living community, which meant cleaning out his home of over forty years and putting it on the market. My husband and I flew up to upstate New York to commence the initial sorting process. During our first sweep of the house, my husband encountered the locked closet containing the aforementioned "Navy Swords." After a little jimmying with his Swiss Army knife, he got in, and I moved on to the next room.

I can still see the look on my husband's face when he emerged from the closet. He looked like he had seen a ghost and told me I did not want to go in the closet. Well, now I really wanted to go in.

You see, my uncle was a gay man, and let's just say he seemed to have had a lot of fun. We never talked about it, and I never asked—I respected his privacy. What he did in his own time was none of my business. Unfortunately, though, now it had become my business. I won't go into the gory details, but let's just say that nobody should have to see what I saw regarding a close relative. My husband and I put on gloves, emptied the entire contents of his closet into a Hefty bag, drove to a liquor store, tossed it in the dumpster out back, and then went inside to buy some booze.

You wouldn't believe the stuff I find in people's homes when my team and I help clean out a decedent's home: sex toys, naughty pictures, used lingerie, pornography, collections of bootleg burned CDs with titles written in Sharpie.

Now, I know we've talked a lot about items nobody wants, but let's stop to consider the things you really don't want your children or family to find. Are there photos, notes, or other belongings that would be embarrassing for you or for them? No judgment here—to each their own, right? However, if you'd rather not contribute to a family member's spontaneous, sudden blindness, it's time to make a plan for their swift removal upon your death.

Maybe you and your BFF Brenda could pinky promise to dispose of each other's collection—whoever goes first? Think of it as predetermining a "designated driver" before things get messy. If that feels like too much pressure, perhaps you could store your items in a box labeled "DESTROY UPON MY DEATH." Either way, take the time to plan for their disposal or leave instructions with someone you trust to handle your literal Pandora's Box.

—— 🪦 ——

NOT JUST A STUFFADEMIC WE'RE FACING—A FULL-BLOWN JUNKADEMIC

The volume of items people accumulate over a lifetime can be staggering, and it's not only the treasured collectibles like Hummel figurines or antique furniture that we're talking about. Often, it's the sheer amount of what many might dismiss as junk that amazes me the most. This isn't limited to those who might lean toward hoarding—though I'm no psychologist, the difficulty for those left to sort through these mountains of miscellany is something I know all too well. It's not just about the emotional weight of sorting a loved one's belongings, but the real costs involved.

For instance, picture this: I had a client whose late father seemed to have been preparing for a Tupperware apocalypse. His basement was a fortress, walled with stacks of plastic containers once home to everything from deli delights to margarine. Seriously, what was the game plan here? An impromptu potluck for 500?

And then there's the more quaint collector type. One client found her mother's extensive collection of Sucrets boxes—not filled with lozenges, but an assortment of buttons, bobby pins, and what I suspect were the lost hopes and dreams of single socks. It's like a tiny museum of everyday life but with none of the charm you'd hope for.

But sometimes, what we uncover goes beyond the quirky or quaint. Sometimes, these collections can verge on the hazardous. During an estate cleanout for Aaron, whose stepfather—a doctor—had recently passed, we encountered items that shifted our task from a simple clear-out to a potential safety hazard. Amidst the ordinary, we found a cache of medications, including fentanyl patches, which were legal and prescribed but needed careful disposal. In the basement, a tackle box not filled with fishing gear but vials of ketamine and Demerol, complete with syringes, was discovered. This finding required us to step back and call in a professional remediation team to handle the removal safely.

These instances highlight the unpredictable nature of clearing out an estate. While many finds are innocuous, the occasional discovery of dangerous items poses serious questions about safety and proper disposal. It's a stark reminder of the breadth of what can accumulate in a home and the importance of preparing for the unexpected. By knowing who to call and what steps to take, we can prevent these potential dangers from falling into the wrong hands.

—— ⚰ ——

PRACTICAL TIPS FOR DECLUTTERING BEFORE IT'S TOO LATE

As an after loss professional, I've witnessed firsthand the complexities involved in estate cleanouts. It's seldom a straightforward task, largely because my role extends beyond the logistical; I also navigate the emotional terrain of decluttering with my clients. The guilt is palpable and multifaceted—guilt about what to do with belongings, uncertainty over the value of items, and discomfort from not wanting, not having space for, or simply not needing these items anymore. There's also the deeper guilt that feels like a betrayal: discarding a loved one's cherished possessions can feel akin to erasing parts of the person themselves.

My own experience came sharply into focus after my mom died, leaving behind a lifetime of memories to sort through. I spent six intense weeks combing through every corner of her home, making heart-wrenching decisions about what to keep, sell, or let go.

One particularly poignant day, I stumbled upon a box filled with artifacts from my parent's wedding over forty years ago. Among these treasures was a bag of rice—rice that my grandmother had painstakingly collected from the ground after it was thrown at my newlywed parents. Holding that bag, I found myself caught between laughter and tears, cursing under my breath. This rice, a seemingly mundane relic, had been part of one of their happiest days. Throwing it away felt like a desecration, yet keeping it felt absurd. It was just rice, but it had touched their lives at such a significant moment.

This emotional conflict is common. Many clients fear that by discarding physical items, they're somehow also discarding the memories attached to them. The anxiety and procrastination that ensue are not unusual, nor are they easy to overcome.

Is eliminating this guilt entirely possible? No. Can it be mitigated? Absolutely. It begins by understanding that while the objects associated with our loved ones are precious, the memories are not solely contained within these items. They live within us—stories and legacy far beyond the physical remnants of a past life.

Personal property distribution can be a source of tension and guilt, but it doesn't have to be. After having cleaned out five of my relative's houses, including one that had been in my family since 1890, I know firsthand how emotionally difficult and agonizing this can be. Here are a couple of tips:

Downsize now. If there are family heirlooms or sentimental items that are to be bequeathed to specific family members, friends, or organizations, do it now. Don't wait until you're gone.

Experience the joy of gifting these special items today.

Take a photo of any keepsake, treasured object, or family heirloom that your family cannot keep or move with them, and have it framed or digitally stored. Alternatively, create a special gift modeled after it.

Create an inventory. Start by cataloging your possessions. Knowing exactly what you have clarifies decisions about what to keep, discard, or pass on.

Communicate and discuss your inventory with your family. Often, they may express interest in items you were unaware held sentimental value to them. This open dialogue can ensure meaningful items are cherished and unnecessary ones are let go without regret.

Evaluate and prioritize items based on their practical use and emotional significance.

Consider the real costs of storage. Does the value of these cherished items, both monetary and sentimental, truly outweigh the potential benefits of letting go? If you choose to hold on to them, will your family members be able to recoup the return on investment of those monthly storage fees?

Seek professional advice early in the process to develop a plan that respects both financial constraints and emotional ties.

What many people fail to grasp is the substantial time and money required to disperse possessions after someone dies. While sudden, unexpected deaths may leave little opportunity for downsizing, it's baffling how some individuals imbue their collections with an overwhelming sense of importance. This reality struck me vividly during a massive estate cleanout I managed for a client who was the executor of his uncle's estate. In his Will, the uncle required that every item, whether a humble pie plate or a grand piece of crystal, be cataloged. My team and I spent weeks documenting over a thousand items—a task as daunting as it was eye-opening. Throughout this process, I was continually struck by the sheer waste of time and resources. What was the purpose of this exhaustive inventory? While we were happy to take on the work, the exercise seemed somewhat futile.

Following the inventory, the family wrestled with decisions about what to keep and what to discard, further draining time, money, and energy. This experience reinforced the idea that while individuals may have different views on the value of their possessions, the responsibility of sorting through these items can become an unintended burden for loved ones. At the end of the day, try to remind yourself that this is just stuff. Even if the item isn't present, the memories always will be.

By proactively decluttering, you can relieve your loved ones of the overwhelming task of sorting through your belongings during a period of grief. This strategy is not only practical but is a critical component of thoughtful legacy planning. Just as we meticulously manage finances and important documents to ensure a smooth transition, deliberately handling physical possessions is equally crucial. By organizing your affairs now, you ensure that your final farewell is as orderly and considerate as every other aspect of your planned departure, preventing your estate from becoming an undue burden on the next generation.

But remember, it's just stuff. These objects don't encapsulate the entirety of a person's life or the depth of our relationships. Sometimes, the best tribute we can offer is not a cramped home filled with relics but a heart full of memories and a legacy of love unburdened by material chains.

— ⚰ —

PROACTIVE GIFTING: HAND OVER THE HEIRLOOMS EARLY

If you're concerned about potential disputes over your cherished collections, consider passing them on to their intended recipients while you're still here. This proactive approach can prevent misunderstandings and ensure that each item is cherished as you intend.

For instance, I once assisted a client, Julia, whose mother had meticulously outlined in her Will exactly which family heirlooms and collectibles should pass directly to Julia, bypassing her stepfather. The mother's intention was clear: these items were to remain within her direct lineage.

Julia requested my presence at her stepfather's house to help facilitate the transfer of these items. Despite my initial reluctance—I'm no moving expert—I agreed to help her. When we arrived, the atmosphere was tense; her stepfather seemed to watch our every move like a hawk.

As we packed the items, which were neatly displayed in a glass cabinet, I felt less like a consultant and more like a referee or mediator armed with bubble wrap instead of a whistle. The situation became particularly strained when it came to a set of tableware that Julia's mother had also earmarked for her—a set her stepfather was currently using for his lunch. Sensing the potential for conflict, I advised Julia to forgo the tableware for the sake of peace.

However, a seemingly insignificant Oneida silverplate candy dish became the flashpoint. As Julia reached for it, her stepfather immediately protested, claiming it as his own. Despite its minimal value, the emotional stakes escalated quickly into a heated argument. After several minutes of back-and-forth, Julia conceded, leaving the dish behind to avoid further conflict.

This experience underscores the importance of clear communication and perhaps the wisdom of transferring meaningful items ahead of time. Waiting until after a loved one's passing can often complicate what should be a straightforward process turning the division of even low-value items into a battleground of wills and emotions.

So, if you treasure your peace of mind as much as your Precious Moments figurines, consider preemptively placing them in the hands of those who value them most. It's not just about preventing disputes; it's about ensuring your legacy is preserved in the way you envision without leaving a trail of family strife in your wake.

A PLEDGE TO THE FUTURE

I swear, as long as I have a say in it, I will not leave behind a house stuffed to the gills for my family to sort through—a potential minefield of stress and squabbles over who gets what. The last thing I want is for a "Dead People's Things For Sale" sign to be my final legacy.

But I know it's not that easy. I have no idea how my children will feel about tossing my belongings into the garbage after I've crossed the great rainbow bridge. Each item could represent a cherished memory, a milestone, or, to them, a story worth preserving. But I also know that these objects can feel like chains that tie them to a past they do not relate to or have space for in their streamlined, modern existences.

To bridge this gap, it's essential for both generations to engage in open, empathetic dialogues about the emotional and practical aspects of inheritance. Here are a few strategies that might help:

- **Legacy Discussions** Facilitate conversations about what really constitutes a legacy. Are they the physical items, or the stories and memories associated with them? Encourage families to share stories about the items, which can sometimes lead to a greater appreciation or a mutual agreement on how to handle them.

- **Selective Keepsakes** Instead of holding onto every item, encourage heirs to choose one or a few pieces that have personal significance. This allows for the preservation of memories without the overwhelming burden of numerous possessions.

- **Modern Memorials** Consider creative ways to preserve memories, like digital photo albums or custom artwork that incorporates materials or themes from inherited items, making the old treasures part of new creations.

- **Professional Appraisal** Before deciding what to keep, sell, or donate, consider getting a professional appraisal from a USPAP-compliant appraiser for certain items or collections. This can provide a reality check on the actual value of possessions, which might be less than expected.

By proactively addressing these concerns, we can ensure that the process of managing an estate is not just about unloading physical items but about respecting and honoring the past in a way that enriches the future. This mindful approach not only eases the burden on the next generation but also honors the legacy in a dignified and loving manner, ensuring that the transition is as respectful and organized as every other aspect of a well-planned departure.

CHAPTER 07
DYING IS EXPENSIVE AF: THE HIGH COST OF THE HEREAFTER

Dying is expensive, and not just in terms of dollars and cents. The end of life brings with it a cascade of burdens that reach far beyond the financial—though those are substantial. There are the time costs, mental costs, sentimental costs, and sometimes, the profound cost to family relationships. And then, there's the gravity of mistakes—errors made in the haze of grief and haste that can ripple out with lasting consequences.

———— ⚰ ————

THE FINANCIAL COST

Death: the final frontier, or so it's been called. But before you embark on that ultimate journey, let's talk about the earthly matters left behind, specifically the bills. It turns out that exiting stage left is not only a profound event but also a pricey one. Who knew the afterlife had such a steep cover charge?

Funeral Costs

After my mom's death, we found ourselves at the familiar funeral home that had serviced not just our father's disposition but also several of my husband's family members. Half-jokingly, I mused about the possibility of a loyalty program—perhaps a buy-one-get-one offer on urns, akin to a buy-one-get-one free Blizzard at Dairy Queen.

Our mother had left clear directives: cremation, with her remains divided—a portion in an urn and buried next to our father in the fancy cemetery in Knoxville with the rest of her family, some scattered in Harriman's old historic cemetery with the extended generations of family, and the rest in the backyard at the old family home. My sister and I also planned to keep some of her, effectively splitting her ashes into fifths.

Walking into a funeral home post-loss feels akin to an emergency car purchase when you're already late for work. The vulnerability is palpable. While I'm not saying that funeral directors are inherently predatory, the industry isn't known for affordability. Let's be honest: there's not usually a coupon for caskets in the Savvy Saver.

And price comparisons? Good luck. The Federal Trade Commission, which oversees regulations for the death care industry, is currently considering an update to the Funeral Rule that might require funeral homes to post their pricing information online. The original rule from 1984, amended last in 1994, predates widespread internet use and only mandates funeral homes to share pricing over the phone. Imagine needing to visit or call multiple car dealerships just to learn their prices—absurd, right?

This lack of transparency exacerbates the stress during a time when consumers are least equipped to navigate complex purchasing decisions.

As we sat in the somber office, browsing through urn options, my sister and I explained to the director that we needed one container to scatter my mother's ashes and three others for safekeeping. Without missing a beat, he presented the "perfect" solution—a container resembling a powdered Coffeemate creamer dispenser with a swiveling lid, priced at the princely sum of $180. I nearly choked on my coffee.

Ironically, we'd swung by Chick-fil-A earlier and still had the container from our chicken minis. I half-jokingly suggested, "Can we just rinse this out and use it instead?" Let's just say that Mr. Funeral Director wasn't amused.

The container, adorned with doves, was apparently biode-gradable—a fact that did little to sweeten the bitter pill of its cost. Paying $180 to house bone and ash for a week before scattering her in the wind seemed utterly preposterous. How ridiculous it felt to ponder over such an expense for something destined for a swift goodbye.

The conversation that unfolded was as absurd as it was enlightening, revealing the bizarre reality of commercial-ized grief. It underscored a profound truth: the logistics of death are not only emotionally taxing but bewilderingly costly, compelling families to make rapid financial decisions in moments of peak vulnerability. Little did I know that I could have shopped elsewhere for a less expensive scatter-ing urn and that the funeral home could not refuse to use it or charge a fee for its use.

In 2023, the average price of a burial was reported at $9,995, marking a 6.1% rise since 2021, as per data from the National Funeral Directors Association (NFDA). This price includes all pre-burial expenses, such as the casket, but excludes costs related to cemetery plots or headstone markers.

For cremations, which include both a container and urn, the median cost stood at $6,280 in 2023, reflecting an 8.1% increase from two years prior. These figures do not account for the expenses of acquiring a cemetery niche and its marker. During this period, the U.S. inflation rate escalated to 13.6%, according to the NFDA, referencing information from the U.S. Department of Labor.

Add to this the variable costs of cemetery plots, which fluctuate based on location and plot size, and the fees for opening and closing the grave, burial permits, grave liners, and perpetual care, and the financial toll of death begins to mount alarmingly. This doesn't even account for the additional expenses like obituaries, death notices, flowers, and other things like the food and beverages for a memorial luncheon.

Little did I know that the succession of rapid financial decisions was just starting. What followed was an onslaught of tasks: probating my mom's estate, emptying her home, and navigating legal complexities across state lines with attorneys in Georgia and Tennessee for her estate and another in New York for my uncle's affairs. Every step seemed to ring up costs like a bachelor's weekend—cha-ching, cha-ching, cha-ching.

Legal and Court Fees

Legal expenses can add up fast when dealing with an estate.

For an estate with minimal complications, you might expect legal costs to fall between $3,500 and $7,000, according to industry estimates. However, things can escalate quickly if there are additional complexities—like a family dispute or multiple properties to manage. In more complicated cases, legal fees can easily soar into the tens of thousands, and in extreme situations, they can go much higher.

For example, I had a client involved in litigation over a contested Will, and the numbers they shared with me were eye-popping. At the time, they had already accumulated over $200,000 in legal fees, and there seemed to be no end in sight. The emotional toll of the dispute was high, and the financial burden was equally significant. This highlights just how important it is to plan ahead and avoid the legal mine-fields that can crop up when there's ambiguity or conflict within an estate.

This is an especially hard pill to swallow if you think you've done everything you can to prevent probate in the first place. You see, after going through probate with my mom's estate, I was going to do everything in my power to prevent from having to do it a second time.

Following my mom's death and armed with a financial Power of Attorney, we believed we understood his financial landscape thoroughly and tried to meticulously organize my uncle's affairs. On paper, his final affairs seemed straightfor-ward: assets were clearly accounted for, beneficiaries were up-to-date (or so we thought), his real estate and person-al property had been liquidated, and he had comfortably downsized into a senior living community designed to cater to his escalating needs.

However, after his death, a call to one of his financial institutions unveiled a startling oversight: an unnamed beneficiary on one of his retirement accounts—a crucial detail that slipped through the cracks despite our diligent preparations. This was not just any account but one necessitating a distinct process for beneficiary designation, diverging from the others. This was news to us.

Consequently, we found ourselves ensnared in the probate process, an ordeal we had desperately sought to avoid, armed with lessons from handling my mother's estate. This particular struggle unfolded in New York, one of the most expensive states to die in, according to PolicyGenius. In our case, accessing an $80,000 account ended up costing us over $10,000 in legal and probate court fees. The takeaway lesson? Ensure every account specifically has named and correct beneficiaries. I had assumed that this could be uniformly done across all accounts with each company or custodian—in this instance, Vanguard—but I learned that different accounts might require distinct processes for naming beneficiaries.

Medical Bills

Many of my clients are shocked and stressed by the medical bills they receive in the mail after their loved one has died. You see, if you die in a hospital or after a long illness, there's a good chance you might leave behind some unpaid medical bills. But who's on the hook for these debts?

The quick answer: not your family. Instead, any debts you leave behind, including medical bills, are typically handled by your estate. This means that everything you own at the time of your death may be used to pay off what you owe.

Your estate pays your debts before anything is handed down to your heirs. Take the case of my client, Luke. He was named executor after his Aunt Lucy's death, who had spent her final year battling serious health issues, resulting in multiple hospital and rehab visits. After her death, Luke was overwhelmed by the flood of bills from hospitals, doctors, and physical therapy centers. One staggering bill alone amounted to over $83,000. Luke enlisted my assistance to sort through and understand each bill. Thankfully, through asking more questions, we managed to significantly reduce many of the charges, mainly due to the fact that they had incorrectly filed her healthcare insurance. However, the total still represented a significant portion of the estate's debts.

Sometimes, if there's not enough in the estate to cover everything, the outstanding debts can be written off. However, there are exceptions:

- **Cosigned Medical Bills** If someone else signed any agreement to pay your medical bills, they might be held responsible.
- **Community Property States** If you live in a community property state like California or Texas, your spouse might be responsible for your debts, even those they didn't personally incur.

The Consumer Financial Protection Bureau reports that surviving spouses are more likely to have outstanding medical debts than others, and the amounts tend to be higher as well. On average, new widows and widowers face around $28,749 in unpaid medical bills, significantly more than the $15,785 reported by others in the general population.

Remember, rules can vary significantly depending on where you live, so it's a smart move to talk to an estate planning attorney to understand exactly what applies in your case. This way, you can plan ahead and possibly avoid leaving your family with financial surprises.

Utilities, Household Bills, And Cleanout Costs

The costs of unfurnishing a house after death can include:

- **Cleaning and Moving** The executor is responsible for cleaning the home, organizing personal property, and disposing of the decedent's personal items as needed.
- **Junk Removal** The executor may also hire professionals to assist with the emotionally challenging and physically demanding task of junk removal.
- **Utility Services** The executor will need to pay utility services to maintain the property while it's being cleared out and prepared for sale.
- **Auctioning and Selling Valuables** The process of auctioning or selling valuable or collectible items may incur costs. These can include fees for hiring an appraiser to accurately value items and potential charges for selling on consignment, where revenue is split between the estate and the consignment service.
- **Professional Services** The executor may need to hire professionals to help with tasks like listing real estate, making home repairs, or maintaining the yard.

These expenses should ideally be covered by the estate using the decedent's assets. If the assets aren't enough, the executor or a family member may need to pay costs out of pocket until they can be reimbursed. Additionally, some of these expenses, like house clearance, might be covered by the decedent's insurance policy.

Debts and Liabilities

As we talked about in Chapter 5, not knowing the decedent's assets and liabilities is a huge blind spot. While finding unknown accounts is usually a welcome surprise, finding out about debts is not, especially when they have no idea.

One of the biggest questions I get from clients is, do I have to pay off debts? Many people think that they will be personally liable for their loved one's debts, and while that's usually not true unless they cosigned a loan with them, the estate usually is responsible.

When a person dies, settling their debts becomes a crucial task, handled primarily through their estate. According to guidelines from the Consumer Financial Protection Bureau, debts are typically settled using the decedent's remaining assets.

Here's a more detailed look at how this process unfolds:

Estate Responsibility Initially, the estate is responsible for paying off any debts. If the estate lacks sufficient funds, most debts are generally not transferred to relatives unless they co-signed or are joint account holders.

Survivor Responsibilities Surviving family members are usually not liable for the decedent's debts unless they are joint account holders, co-signers, or married, or live in community property states where such obligations might legally transfer to them.

Debt Collectors' Interactions While debt collectors may contact survivors, they cannot imply that survivors are personally liable for the debts, except under specific legal situations. It's important for survivors to know their rights under the Fair Debt Collection Practices Act, which protects them from harassment and abuse by collectors.

Legal Guidance It's often advisable to consult with an estate or probate lawyer to clarify any responsibilities and ensure the estate is settled correctly. For those who cannot afford a lawyer, legal aid societies or eldercare locator services may offer support.

No Estate or Insufficient Assets If there are no assets left to cover the debts, typically, these debts will go unpaid. This scenario can vary slightly by state laws regarding estate and debt settlement.

By understanding these key points, executors and family members can navigate the complexities of settling debts after a loved one's death more effectively, ensuring that they comply with legal requirements and protect their own financial interests.

The Loss of Income

My dad died at the age of forty-eight, having practiced medicine for just eleven years, after a belated start to his career. His early college days were interrupted when he was drafted into the U.S. Army during the peak of the Vietnam War—a conflict he couldn't avoid. My parents married while he served, and shortly thereafter, he was deployed to Vietnam. Upon returning, he resumed his academic pursuits, entering medical school in Philadelphia—the same year I was born.

After completing his internship and residency, our family relocated to a small town in dire need of medical services.

His practice flourished quickly, often seeing him manage up to fifty patients daily, with his days beginning and ending at the hospital.

Cancer first struck my father when I was thirteen. After a brief remission when I was fifteen, it returned more aggressively and then ultimately claimed his life the following year. My mom had forsaken her librarian career to manage his solo practice, so when he died, our family faced the abrupt end of both incomes. Thankfully, my father had made prudent financial plans due to his substantial earnings as a doctor. However, the sudden financial uncertainty was deeply troubling for my mom, as it wasn't just about the income lost but the future financial security that was abruptly truncated.

This story echoes the experiences of many others, like my friend Jessica, who faced a sudden upheaval when her partner Brian passed away unexpectedly. Brian, who was on the cusp of stepping into a promising new job that would have significantly improved their financial stability, died before he could start. Jessica, left with three young children and no life insurance in place, faced immediate financial hardship—a reminder of how crucial planning for the unexpected can be. Brian's untimely death not only removed their primary income source but also left them dealing with additional heartaches, like their car being repossessed, a stark and visible sign of their changed circumstances.

THE TIME COST

Brace yourselves because settling an estate isn't just a chore—
it's a bureaucratic ultramarathon. It's often portrayed as a
quick task, but in reality, it can be a long journey. According
to EstateExec, the process requires an average of roughly
570 hours of effort by an executor. Further data from Caring.
com suggests the ordeal can drag on for nine to eighteen
months, and another study says families invest twenty hours
a week for over a year to settle all financial affairs. Imagine
the commitment required: an executor might spend over
100 distinct tasks wrestling with everything from court documents to estate taxes. That's a significant chunk of time that
could otherwise be spent with loved ones, focusing on work,
or enjoying much-needed downtime.

Think of estate management as a second full-time job, one
you never applied for. Executors often find themselves mired
in endless tasks: canceling services, notifying banks, distributing assets, and wading through the molasses of probate—
all while the clock ticks on.

In the weeks leading up to my mother's death, my life felt
like a circus act—balancing hospital visits with a demanding
new job, nights spent in hospital chairs, and mornings filled
with family duties. With no paid leave accrued, I was skating
on thin ice with my employer's patience.

Oh, and let's not forget the irony—thick enough to cut with a
knife—a bitter, dry cake, if you will. After spending almost a
decade at Emory University, the last of my years in the School
of Medicine, I had accrued lots of time off and had daily

access to some of the best doctors out there. Unaware of the catastrophe that lurked around the corner, I jumped ship to a higher-paying gig in healthcare philanthropy across town. From my mom's hospital room, I could literally see my old office—my former command center. There I was, staring out at it, pondering the cruel twist of fate that had me missing the perks I'd left behind.

Thanks a bunch, Murphy's Law.

When my mom died, the administrative burdens multiplied like rabbits. The responsibilities didn't respect office hours; they barged right into my daily grind at work. I recall being jolted out of a workday reverie during a meeting, feeling like a student caught daydreaming by a sharp-eyed teacher. Most estate-related tasks need handling during standard business hours, which complicates things even for those of us with regular office jobs.

Eventually, the relentless pace forced my hand. After eight months of high-wire multitasking, I took a dramatic step: a leave of absence from my career. I had never paused my career, not even after either of my children was born, above and beyond the twelve-week maternity leave. Yet, here I was, taking an indefinite sabbatical not to usher in and enjoy a pause with my new bundle of joy but to wrestle with the grim reaper's paperwork—a real plot twist from life's usual script.

The executor role shared with my sister following our uncle's death consumed our lives— affecting our jobs, marriages, and time with our children. It's a role that transcends legal responsibilities; it's a full-time commitment with no punch-out clock.

Interestingly, it's often the oldest daughter who finds herself at the helm of estate affairs. According to caregiving.com, the typical caregiver is a forty-nine-year-old woman who balances a full-time job with around twenty hours of unpaid caregiving each week. This predisposition to caregiving often means that when the executor's responsibilities are delegated, they naturally fall to women already seasoned in managing care.

Consider the case of my client Abby, who had been the primary caregiver for her mother during her prolonged illness. Abby, the middle child yet the eldest daughter, not only shouldered the caregiving burden but also became in charge of her eighteen-year-old sister's care after her mother died. A teacher and seventh-grade volleyball coach, Abby's day was a continuous whirl from 7 a.m. to 4 p.m., leaving little to no room for the demanding tasks of an executor. Opening an estate checking account—a seemingly simple task—became a monumental challenge. The bank's rigid hours clashed with her non-stop schedule, and the emotional weight of the process was overwhelming. Abby found herself paralyzed by the responsibilities to the point of disengaging entirely until summer break, which allowed her some breathing room to manage these perfunctory tasks.

Now, please know that this narrative isn't about igniting a gender debate; rather, it's about equipping the women who frequently find themselves at the epicenter of these responsibilities. By shedding light on these common challenges, perhaps we can smooth the path for those who invariably find themselves "holding the bag," ensuring they have the necessary tools and knowledge to navigate these turbulent waters effectively.

THE MENTAL IMPACT

Attempting to settle an estate while in the throes of grief seems like it would be a lot like attempting to drive while under the influence. Just as alcohol impairs judgment, slows reaction times, and blurs vision, grief clouds judgment, delays responses, and obscures the mental clarity needed for effective decision-making. Executors are required to make financial decisions, interpret legal documents, and negotiate with beneficiaries—all tasks that demand high cognitive function, which grief compromises.

Do you recall that commercial from the late 1980s of a Public Service Announcement (PSA) featuring a frying egg to depict the brain under the influence of drugs? Its iconic tagline, "This is your brain on drugs," captured the concept of mental impairment vividly. Imagine a similar PSA for grief, but instead of a frying pan, picture a blender. Inside, thoughts and emotions whirl into chaos, symbolizing the tumultuous mental state grief induces.

Remember Abby, whose story I shared above? After weeks of silence, she finally reached out, apologizing for her disappearance. "I'm sorry I stopped responding," she confessed. "At some point, it just became too much, and I needed to step back." Her honesty about needing a break was a profound reminder of the mental load grief can impose.

The overwhelming pressure to make urgent, impactful decisions during such a vulnerable time adds another layer of complexity to an executor's responsibilities. They must navigate the legal landscape, fulfill the decedent's wishes, and manage family dynamics, often under the watchful and sometimes critical eyes of other family members. This pressure can exacerbate stress and emotional fatigue, leading to decision fatigue, where the quality of decision-making can decrease after a long session of decision-making.

THE SENTIMENTAL CASUALTIES OF DEATH

When a loved one dies, the physical remnants of their life become more than mere objects; they transform into vessels of memory, each holding a story, a moment, or a feeling. This sentimental toll involves navigating a minefield of memories with every item that belonged to the decedent. Deciding the fate of grandma's teapot or dad's favorite recliner can unleash a fresh wave of grief, proving that sometimes, objects aren't just things—they're emotional landmines.

The logistical and financial burdens of dealing with an estate can overshadow efforts to preserve sentimental memories and family traditions. As families rush to settle estates, important stories and artifacts, like grandma's handwritten recipes or dad's tool collection, might be hastily divided, sold, or even discarded, sometimes regretfully so.

Physical items such as family photos, heirlooms, and personal letters carry immense sentimental value and can become focal points of memory for a family. Unfortunately, without a plan, these items can be lost, mishandled, or damaged during the whirlwind process of estate settlement. Consider digitizing old photos, creating memory books, or distributing duplicates among family members to ensure these memories persist.

Loss of Historical Family Knowledge Often, the stories behind objects or traditions go undocumented, residing only in the minds of family members. When a loved one dies, particularly a matriarch or patriarch, there is a risk that this invaluable family history may vanish with them. Encourage family members to share stories, perhaps recording them during family gatherings, to preserve this oral history for future generations.

Emotional Landmines in Family Dynamics The emotional weight of distributing a decedent's belongings can strain family relationships, sometimes leading to disputes that last long after the estate is settled. These objects can symbolize different things to different family members, leading to clashes over who gets what. Clear communication and mediation, possibly guided by a professional, can help navigate these emotionally charged decisions.

Creating New Traditions While the loss of a loved one can alter family dynamics, it also provides an opportunity to create new traditions. Incorporating items from a loved one into new practices can help keep their memory alive and aid in the healing process. For example, using dad's favorite fishing rods on annual family trips or grandma's quilts during holiday gatherings can turn items of grief into symbols of continuity and love.

After losing our parents, my sister and I started a new tradition: "Crab Legs for Christmas." It was our way of hitting the reset button, creating something meaningful for us in their absence.

——— ⚰ ———

THE LOSS OF FAMILY RELATIONSHIPS

The emotional toll of estate disputes often extends beyond financial losses, deeply affecting family relationships. The saying, "Where there's a Will, there's a relative," humorously underscores how inheritances can unearth latent familial conflicts and bring distant relatives out of the woodwork. The distribution of assets, a process loaded with emotional significance, can sometimes leave family members feeling marginalized or wronged. This tension can transform a dignified mourning process into something resembling a soap opera, complete with betrayals and dramatic reversals fit for daytime TV.

For instance, I've encountered numerous stories in my practice about the fallout from inheritance conflicts. Many share tales of siblings who no longer speak post-settlement—a profound loss that can rival the grief of losing a family member.

Shortly after our mother died, my sister found out she was pregnant. While it was a wonderful bit of news during a tough year, it meant she couldn't be deeply involved in settling our mother's estate. I've always been someone who takes charge—once, a personality test even compared my work style to that of a "dictatorial steamroller." It was a bit harsh but accurate in some ways. I was driven to manage the estate efficiently, but this sometimes led me to make decisions without consulting my sister. Caught up in the momentum, I occasionally overlooked her perspectives, leading to some tense conversations. While I felt her appreciation was lacking, I had to admit communication could have been better on my part.

Similarly, a client named Emma faced challenges while executing her mother's estate. Despite her best efforts to manage the estate responsibly, a necessary yet uncommunicated financial decision led to significant friction with her brother, George. After he covered a crucial tax bill to avoid penalties, Emma's delay in reimbursement due to her demanding job schedule strained their relationship. I advised her to settle the debt promptly to prevent further damage. Such miscommunications are common and highlight the need for clear, consistent communication among beneficiaries.

THE COST OF MISTAKES— THE OOPS FACTOR

Lastly, the cost of mistakes—because grief wasn't enough of a challenge. Missteps while settling an estate can range from the "Oops, I did it again" kind to the "I think I need a lawyer" kind, each adding its own special layer of complexity to an already delightful process.

Mistake #1: Thinking It's a Sprint, Not a Marathon
Big surprise—being an executor is a marathon wrapped in a bureaucratic bow. It can be a big commitment, and diving in without understanding the sheer breadth of what you're taking on is like trying to bake a soufflé without knowing how to turn on the oven. Understand the scope, get your emotional armor on, and brace yourself for the long haul.

Mistake #2: Playing Eenie, Meenie, Miny, Mo with Probate Attorneys

When my mom passed away, I ended up with an attorney who came highly recommended but was semi-retired. His gradual withdrawal from professional life meant that my mom's estate dragged on for years, turning simple legal proceedings into a marathon. Lesson learned? Never just settle for the first option or a recommendation without digging a little deeper.

For my uncle's estate, I went with the first attorney who called me back—a decision born of urgency rather than prudence. Treat finding an attorney like online dating—shop around, ask the hard questions, and don't settle until you find "The One" who can handle your unique brand of family crazy.

An experienced estate attorney can significantly streamline the legal maze and prevent costly pitfalls. Questions to ask might include:

- **Specialization** "Is trust and estate law your main focus?"
- **Experience** "Have you managed cases similar to mine?"
- **Communication** "How will you keep me updated on progress?"
- **Fees** "Can you break down your fee structure?"
- **Requirements** "What documents and information do you need from me?"
- **Timeline** "What's a realistic timeline for my case?"

Taking these steps can help ensure that the attorney you choose is not only capable but also a good fit for your specific needs, turning a potentially fraught experience into a manageable one.

Mistake #3: Disorganization Nation

To ensure a more accurate and efficient estate settlement, I strongly recommend creating a spreadsheet to keep track of debts, assets, and expenses. Organize financial documents, create a comprehensive inventory of assets and debts, and maintain clear records. Furthermore, if you're disposing of personal property, gather information, do research, and take pictures before selling, liquidating, or distributing to beneficiaries. These simple steps will save you time, money, and potential disputes down the road.

Mistake #4: Lone Wolf Syndrome

Why try to settle a loved one's affairs alone when there are experts who specialize in this? Why slog through estate settlements solo when there are pros who eat this stuff for breakfast? In today's hustle culture, it's tempting to shoulder it all—bad idea. Professionals who specialize in estate settlements bring a treasure trove of expertise to dodge the legal lingo and sidestep potential pitfalls. And yes, this is a not-so-subtle nudge to consider hiring an after loss professional. Hey, sometimes a little self-promo is necessary, right?

Mistake #5: Radio Silence with Beneficiaries

Playing the silent game with beneficiaries is about as effective as trying to sneak a sunrise past a rooster. I get it; folks are busy these days, and the last thing someone may remember to do on their never-ending to-do list is send out an update to beneficiaries. However, a savvy attorney once laid it out for me: being an executor is like being the bouncer at the bank vault. Everyone's eyeing the inheritance and surprise—money can make folks a tad irrational.

As the executor, your job is to manage the Will's execution, not to hoard secrets. Remember the mistake I made of not keeping my sister in the loop? Making sure everyone is informed can help avert major family drama. Even updates like "things are running behind schedule" or "we've hit a snag" are better than silence. After all, no one can read minds—not yours or the dearly departed's.

—— 🪦 ——

THE FINAL CHECKLIST—NAVIGATING THE PRICEY PATH OF PARTING

As we wrap up this whirlwind tour through the costly corridors of the hereafter, I'm offering you, dear reader, a distilled dose of directives to dodge the financial pitfalls of death. Here's my prescription to keep your affairs in shipshape:

Educate Yourself Knowledge is your ally, and ignorance is your adversary. Understand the laws in your state and what applies specifically to your situation—be it Wills, Trusts, or the magical realms of tax implications.

Plan Proactively Don't wait for the storm to hit before fixing the roof. Set up your estate plan early, update it regularly, and make sure it reflects your current wishes and life situation. Yes, it's about as fun as watching paint dry, but so is dealing with a mess you could have avoided.

Communicate Clearly Channel your inner broadcaster and keep all relevant parties in the loop. Secrets might make for good movies, but they're disastrous in estate planning. Keep your family and designated executors informed about your plans and any changes to them.

Hire Wisely When it comes to legal help, don't skimp. Find a trusted and experienced attorney who specializes in estate planning. They're worth their weight in gold for the headaches they'll save you down the line.

Prepare for the Emotional Journey Settling an estate is not just a logistical challenge but an emotional gauntlet. Understand the psychological toll it can take and prepare yourself and your loved ones for the journey.

Consider Mediation Before disputes turn into catastrophes, consider facilitated discussions. Sometimes, a neutral third party can smooth over the bumps that emotional investments create.

Keep a Sense of Humor When all else fails, remember to laugh. It's okay to find humor in the absurdity of some of these processes. After all, what are life and death but the ultimate cosmic joke?

By taking these steps, you're not just preparing to depart this world; you're ensuring your exit is as graceful as your life was meaningful. Arm yourself with knowledge, fortify your legacy with careful planning, and maybe, just maybe, you can turn the final curtain into a standing ovation rather than a dramatic intermission.

CHAPTER 08
THINGS NOT TO DO: FRIENDS DON'T LET FRIENDS NAME CO-EXECUTORS

Imagine waking up tomorrow thrust into a job where your first task is to build a 10,000-foot bridge. Or maybe you're wheeling into an operating room to perform open-heart surgery. Or perhaps you're sitting down to hammer out the finer points of a multi-billion dollar corporate merger. Feeling a cold sweat coming on? Yep, that's the stomach-churning reality for many unwitting executors thrust into their roles without so much as a "how do you do?"

Having been through the executor wringer twice—once for my mother and once for my uncle—I've seen firsthand that the preparation most people provide their executors is, to put it bluntly, craptastic.

After my stints as co-executor, I resonated deeply with my mother's colorful expression: I felt like I'd been "shot at and missed, shit on and hit." A bit crude, perhaps, but nothing captures the wear-and-tear of executor duties quite like down-home wisdom.

Here's the gritty reality: settling my mother's estate took a staggering seven and a half years. My uncle's estate? A speedy two and a half years. Back when I was still navigating these legal labyrinths, I left a job I'd only been at for eight months—not because it was a bad fit, but because the crushing weight of executor responsibilities left me no other choice.

I was juggling the sale of five properties and managing care for my ailing uncle, all while trying to maintain my roles as an employee, mother, wife, and—speaking candidly—a sane person. As I shared before, the average executor can devote over 500 hours to settling an estate. My marathon? Just as many cramps as running twenty-six miles, along with a decade of twists, turns, and hurdles.

These personal trials led me to establish AfterLight, a venture born from the conviction that while we can't eliminate the pain of loss, we can certainly streamline the logistical nightmares that often amplify it. My mission? To ensure that no one else has to learn the hard way. Being an executor can sometimes feel like being a contestant on a reality show where every challenge is a crisis.

DEMYSTIFYING THE SUPER EXECUTOR MYTH

Repeat after me: *my executor is not a magical unicorn.* In other words, your executor isn't a superhero. They don't wear capes, they don't have magical powers, and they certainly aren't endowed with a supernatural ability to juggle the myriad of tasks estate settlement throws their way. Instead, they are very much human—extraordinary perhaps in their commitment but not in their capabilities.

Here's a quick reality check on what it really takes to be not just a good executor but a functional one:

- **Organizational Prowess** They must manage deadlines, keep track of documents, and think strategically about both immediate tasks and future implications.
- **Financial Literacy** A solid understanding of financial matters is crucial, particularly when handling estates with complex assets.
- **Legal Acumen** They don't need to be lawyers, but a basic understanding of estate structures (like Wills versus Trusts) gives you a definite leg up.
- **Network Navigation** Knowing who to call—from attorneys and accountants to financial advisors—is half the battle.
- **Communication and Decision-Making** Clear, decisive communication is essential, especially when decisions affect multiple stakeholders.

Individually, these skills are manageable, but finding a single person who embodies all these traits? That's asking for a unicorn.

So, let's bust some myths about the presumed superpowers of executors:

- **Mind Reading** Executors can't intuit the wishes of the decedent beyond what's spelled out in legal documents.

- **Financial Wizardry** They manage assets, sure, but don't expect them to multiply inheritances through alchemy.
- **Legal Savviness** While they handle legal documents, they do not substitute lawyers.
- **Antique Appraisal** Executors might oversee valuations, but they're not walking encyclopedias of antique prices.
- **Professional Mediation** They mediate disputes, but they're not necessarily trained conflict resolution specialists.

Remember, setting realistic expectations and preparing your executor with the right tools and information can prevent a lot of heartache. They're steering the ship through stormy waters, not conjuring calm seas.

Remember, no executor has superpowers, but there are proactive steps you can take to set them up for success. Conversely, there are definite missteps you should avoid. Here are a few things you shouldn't do to your executor.

—— ⚰ ——

THE SEVEN DEADLY SINS—WHAT NOT TO DO TO YOUR EXECUTOR

1. Cloak and Dagger Wills: Keeping Secrets from Your Executor

It's genuinely baffling how many people squirrel away their Will like it's a top-secret document. Here's the deal:

"Rachel, my [relative] just passed, and we can't find their Will anywhere. We've searched high and low—nothing. What do we do now?"

Alright, it's time for some tough love. If you're hitting the third or fourth quarter of life or even just living a full life, thinking you're invincible, please wake up and smell the probate court. How exactly do you expect your family to know you've left a Will? They're grieving, not gearing up for a scavenger hunt.

Let me lay it out plainly: hiding your Will or failing to inform your executor and beneficiaries of its existence is one of the most frustrating things you can do to those you leave behind.

Remember my client Paula, whom we talked about in Chapter 2? In her case, Paula received a call that her Uncle Ben had died, not even knowing that he was sick. Ben was a legend in his own right, known for his zest for life and his unwavering confidence that he'd live past 100. This belief was so strong that Paula had no idea whether or not Ben had gotten around to the formality of estate planning.

Ben's accountant had nagged him for years about getting his estate in order, particularly about securing a Will and updating his beneficiaries, but Ben had never confirmed nor denied whether he had made crucial preparations that would have saved his family a lot of trouble.

Fast forward to Ben's death: the morgue calls Paula, scrambling to find any next of kin. Ben had assets scattered across the country, including rental properties with ongoing leases and tenants who knew nothing about his death. Ben's lack of planning thrust Paula into an administrative nightmare.

Her first task? To find Ben's Will—if it even existed. After months of searching with no success, Paula applied to be the administrator of Ben's estate, assuming he hadn't left any instructions. She then learned about a safe deposit box that might contain the Will, but accessing it meant traveling to another state, navigating bureaucratic red tape, and potentially paying to drill open the box—all with no guarantee that a Will was even inside.

What is the moral of the story? Don't be like Ben. If you have a Will, don't hide the fact that you have one. If you're going to take the time to arrange your affairs, make sure the relevant people know about it. A hidden Will is as useful as no Will at all. Don't leave your loved ones with mysteries to solve when they should be mourning. A simple heads-up can spare your family endless headaches and heartaches.

Make sure your executor knows about the Will, its contents, and exactly where to find it. It's not just considerate; it's crucial. Because guess what? If you have taken the time and the money to invest in creating a Will and then your family can't find it, that was a complete waste of energy and cash.

2. Guess Who? Not Informing Your Executor They're It

Remember the TV ads where Ed McMahon surprised unsuspecting folks with a giant check? Those were the kind of surprises people dream about. However, discovering you're an executor without prior knowledge? That's not one of those dreamy surprises.

Finding out you're the executor after someone's death can be as disorienting as it is overwhelming. Imagine getting a call out of the blue that catapults you into the midst of an unexpected and bewildering scenario. This was the reality for Penny, a client who rang me up, bewildered and overwhelmed. Decades had passed—fifty years, to be precise—since Penny had last spoken to her ex-husband, from whom she had long since divorced. Yet, here she was, named as the executor and sole beneficiary of his estate.

The revelation was as shocking as it was puzzling. Not only had they not spoken in half a century, but there also hadn't been any hint of unresolved financial ties or emotional connections that would typically necessitate such an appointment. This posthumous gesture left Penny grappling with a tidal wave of administrative duties and a flood of unanswered questions. Was this a final act of respect, a delayed apology, or, as some might darkly joke, the ultimate post-divorce trick?

Given the dumpster fire that the ex-husband left behind, it seemed to lean towards the latter. Pause for a moment to consider this scenario: suddenly being responsible for the affairs of someone you no longer know. Questions about mortgages, retirement accounts, banking details, car loans, and titles now all fell on her shoulders.

Whatever the intention, Penny found herself catapulted into the role of settling his affairs—a gig involving everything from deciphering decades-old paperwork to contacting a cast of characters, including nieces, nephews, and neighbors, all of whom were strangers to her. This ordeal turned out to be more than a mere logistical headache; it was a psychological jigsaw puzzle that no one could have predicted.

It was almost as if Penny's ex-husband had played a bizarre game of spin the bottle when choosing her as the executor—except the prize was a pile of responsibilities instead of a smooch. To thicken the plot, the man had remarried but still named Penny as the executor. Go figure!

We could spend ages trying to unravel his motives, but really, this oddball scenario serves as a universal reminder: the familiar can become distant, and the distant can suddenly reappear with a to-do list. It's crucial to spend as much time choosing your executor as you do deciding where your assets go. Ask the tough questions. Do they have the right skills? Can they handle the stress? Will they play nice with others involved? Are they savvy enough to manage or even understand the legacy you're leaving behind?

It's essential to discuss your intentions with your chosen executor beforehand to prevent such scenarios. Ensure they understand what being an executor entails and agree to take on this responsibility. This transparency allows them to prepare adequately or decline if they feel unfit for the role, preventing potential distress and complications down the line.

Don't let your Will be a cause for panic or confusion. Just as Ed McMahon made sure winners knew what was coming, give your executor a heads-up. This way, they can step into their role with confidence and clarity, making the estate administration process smoother and more respectful for everyone involved.

3. Estate Jigsaw: Failing to Map Out the Financial Terrain

If I could have any superpower, it would be mind reading. Sadly, that's not on the table, and neither is it for many executors who find themselves clueless about the estates they're supposed to manage. It's like being handed a treasure map with half the landmarks missing. You might find the treasure, or you might end up digging up the whole island.

Take the case of Aaron, previously introduced in Chapter 6, whose stepfather passed away and named him executor in his Will. Good news: Aaron knew about his role. Bad news: he had no clue about the extent of his stepfather's estate—no details on assets, debts, or even where the original Will was stored. His stepfather's estate planning was less "organized filing system" and more "let's throw everything in a drawer and hope for the best."

Aaron's treasure hunt began with a frantic search for the Will and then a painstaking reconstruction of his stepfather's financial life. This wasn't just rummaging through a few drawers; it involved diving into piles of papers and chasing down leads that seemed to materialize out of thin air. Months into this financial detective work, Aaron received a stockholder update addressed to his stepfather that led to the discovery of an asset worth over $500,000 that he hadn't known existed.

This chaotic scavenger hunt is a cautionary tale about the importance of clear communication and thorough documentation. Aaron's ordeal included paying out-of-pocket for court fees, travel expenses, and countless hours spent piecing together financial puzzles—all tasks that could have been simplified or avoided with a better-organized estate plan.

This kind of scenario not only extends the probate process but can significantly increase stress during an already difficult time. Without a clear roadmap of assets and debts, executors can find themselves financially and emotionally drained, grappling with unforeseen challenges that could have been mitigated with a bit of forethought and a lot of transparency.

A Blueprint for Executor Support: To avoid leaving your

executor in the lurch, consider these proactive steps:

- **Comprehensive Documentation** Create and maintain an organized file of all important documents—Wills, Trusts, insurance policies, property deeds, and detailed financial records.
- **Asset and Debt Inventory** Provide a clear, detailed list of all assets and liabilities. This roadmap will save your executor countless hours and unnecessary expenses.
- **Accessible Funds** Ensure there's a small fund accessible to cover immediate posthumous expenses. This might mean setting aside a dedicated account that your executor can access without having to jump through legal hoops.

These steps don't just ease the logistical burden—they're a final act of care, reducing the emotional and financial strain on those you've chosen to finalize your affairs.

4. Double Trouble: The Chaos of Co-Executors

Naming more than one executor without defining their specific duties can lead to conflict and inefficiency, especially if the co-executors have differing opinions on how to handle the estate. While appointing multiple executors might feel like a fair way to distribute responsibilities and prevent accusations of favoritism, my personal experience as a co-executor—twice—taught me it's a recipe for inefficiency and conflict.

Challenges with Co-Executors:

- **Slowed Probate Process** When more than one person is steering the ship, coordinating decisions and signatures can tie up the estate in probate longer than necessary.

- **Imbalanced Workload** Co-executors often find it difficult to split tasks evenly. This can lead to frustration, resentment, or one executor bearing the brunt of the workload.
- **Required Dual Approvals** Every document, check, and decision requires dual signatures, adding layers of complexity to even the simplest tasks.
- **Increased Conflict Potential** Differing views on asset valuation and estate decisions can stir conflict, particularly if pre-existing personal tensions are at play.
- **Risk of Unilateral Decisions** With multiple people involved, there's always the risk that one executor might take actions without the full consensus of the others, potentially derailing the estate settlement process.

Despite having a good relationship and living close to each other, my sister and I faced numerous hurdles as co-executors for our mother's and uncle's estates. Coordination for notarizing documents became a frequent and frustrating routine. Every interaction with attorneys required joint decisions and responses, complicating communications and decision-making. Dealing with institutions often meant roping in my sister for joint authorization, a logistical nightmare that was just about manageable because we were geographically close. Imagine the chaos if we had lived in different states!

To avoid these complications, it's more efficient to appoint a single executor. If you worry about burdening one person with all the responsibilities, consider assigning a backup executor or discussing specific arrangements with your attorney to support the primary executor. This approach simplifies the process, speeds up execution, and minimizes the potential for conflict, ensuring your estate is handled as smoothly and quickly as possible.

5. Leaving a Trail of Random Knick-Knacks in Your Will

Involving specific personal property in your Will might seem thoughtful, but it can morph into a logistical nightmare for your executor. Nothing quite spells chaos like a well-meaning, item-specific bequest. Think you're being thoughtful by earmarking that old-timey stereo for cousin Bob? Think again.

Take my client Joy, who faced unexpected challenges after her father died, leaving her in charge as the executor. Joy's dad, a lawyer by profession, thought he was nailing this estate planning thing. He detailed who gets the family's stereo and weight set—great, right? However, there was a slight plot twist: he had already disposed of these items years before he died. Joy ended up on a wild goose chase, not for treasures, but for some type of proof that these items were long gone. Yes, it was a paper scavenger hunt, thanks to a Will that was more of a time capsule than a useful document.

Why Specific Bequests Might Be Your Will's Kryptonite:

- **Ever-Changing Inventories** What's here today might be sold, lost, or broken tomorrow (or given away at last year's garage sale). Keeping your Will updated with every little change is about as practical as using a typewriter in the age of smartphones.
- **Administrative Nightmares** Expecting your executor to track down the lifecycle of each item is like asking them to play chess in the dark. It's fun in theory but unnecessarily complicated.
- **Emotional Rollercoasters** Disappointment is guaranteed when the promised heirlooms have van-

ished into thin air, leaving beneficiaries feeling more abandoned than treasure hunters who find an empty chest.

Estate Planning Like a Pro

- **Flexibility is Key** Instead of etching item specifics into the granite of your Will, consider a more adaptable approach. Use a Tangible Personal Property Memorandum—less of a formal commitment and more of a living document that can evolve without a lawyer's intervention every time you change your mind.
- **Regular Updates, Less Drama** Keep your list current and communicate any significant changes. Your family and friends will thank you for not turning their grief into a game of "finders keepers."
- **The Memorandum Magic** It's legally valid, easy to update, and doesn't require you to move mountains (or pay hefty legal fees) to adjust. Just sign and date a new list when changes arise, and voilà!

My uncle's Will read like a collector's catalog—meticulously itemizing his antique tubas and piano scrolls. However, he didn't specify their locations or current statuses. Worse yet, some beneficiaries predeceased him or were incapacitated, leading to significant confusion and additional legwork for me as the executor, who had to verify the status of each bequest. This not only created unnecessary work but also prolonged the settlement process.

Keep it simple, keep it updated, and keep your executor in the loop. They'll be juggling enough without having to turn into Indiana Jones on a quest through your past life's relics.

It's essential to consider the practical implications of your estate planning choices. Keeping your Will clear of specific tangible items, unless absolutely necessary, and opting for a personal property memorandum can streamline the executor's duties and prevent potential disputes. Remember, simplicity in planning often translates to easier execution.

6. DIY Disasters: Crafting Chaos with Self-Made Plans

Oh, the internet—our go-to for quick fixes, cat videos, and, yes, even those DIY Will kits that seem like a steal. But here's the scoop: when it comes to estate planning, leaving it to the web might just leave your heirs with a mess. Sure, those online kits are cheap and easy, like fast food for legal needs, but they might not satisfy the unique appetite of your estate. If you ever want to see me squirm, just tell me you whipped up your Will with an online template during a late-night web surf. Cue the full-body cringe from me!

It's encouraging to see innovative solutions addressing America's estate planning gap. Yet, despite the convenience, these online services haven't quite mastered the nuanced art of personalized estate planning, in my personal opinion. Think about it—these sites often give you the basics, like a simple Will, but that's like bringing a feather duster to a fist-fight if you're dealing with anything more complex than a vinyl record collection. A basic Will won't dodge probate or shield you from estate taxes, which can gobble up a chunk of what you leave behind faster than you can say "taxman."

And while these online legal nooks can be handy starting blocks, they can't juggle the intricacies of more elaborate estates. But hey, they're not all bad. Use them as a crash course—Estate Planning 101, if you will—then stride into your lawyer's office armed with questions sharper than a tack. That way, you turn a basic internet primer into a powerhouse prep session for a real, live professional plan. After all, you wouldn't ask Siri to perform surgery, so why trust a website to handle your legacy?

There's a risky allure to DIY estate planning, often sparked by a seemingly harmless tip from a friend or a snippet of advice overheard at a social event. It's easy to be tempted by the anecdotal success stories—like that friend of a friend who said he probate-proofed his estate with a simple trick he learned online. However, these secondhand strategies can quickly turn into a minefield. The same goes for applying DIY planning based on something you heard that a friend's mother's brother's cousin did, a tip you read on Facebook, or advice you gleaned from someone on TikTok dancing to the latest Cardi B track.

Consider the tale of Joseph, a businessman with dealings and debts across the U.S. and Canada. Upon his sudden death, his adult children conducted a basic search for a Will but were pretty sure one didn't exist. Years earlier, Joseph and his parents had executed a DIY estate planning strategy to shield their family home by transferring the deed to Joseph. They believed this transfer would protect the home if they ever needed to enter a nursing home by keeping it from being sold to cover long-term care costs and reducing their assets to qualify for Medicaid long-term care benefits. This preemptive move was intended to safeguard their legacy from potential financial strains.

This well-intentioned strategy backfired when Joseph died unexpectedly, making the house part of his estate. Now, with significant debts looming, creditors had a possible path to place liens against the house, threatening the financial security and residence of Joseph's elderly parents.

This example underscores the risks of makeshift estate planning without professional guidance. The stakes are too high, and the repercussions too severe to leave to chance. If you're considering taking estate planning into your own hands or making significant decisions such as transferring ownership of your home, think carefully and consult with a professional. It's about safeguarding not just your assets but the well-being of those you love. After all, the goal is to ensure your legacy is a blessing, not a landmine.

7. If There's A Quid Pro Quo, Let Them Know

I debated whether to include this as one of the deadly sins, but I think it's important to address the growing reality of family estrangement, its increasing prevalence in society, and my personal interest in discussing the intersection of estrangement and estate planning.

Family estrangement can profoundly affect both those who sever ties and those left behind, often leading to deep feelings of grief and guilt. This is a reality I know all too well, having experienced it personally. Without delving into the painful specifics, the fallout had significant and irreparable ripple effects on my family. In this instance, I had a ringside view of a conditional provision in a Will, which was used as a tool for revenge and manipulation, putting the executor in a real pickle.

Estrangement is increasingly recognized and even normalized in today's society. Why is this happening? More and more, younger generations are prioritizing mental health and personal boundaries, sometimes choosing these over maintaining strained family ties.

The shift towards recognizing the need for healthy personal boundaries has gained substantial media attention. For example, an article in *The New Yorker* titled "Why So Many People Are Going 'No Contact' with Their Parents" discusses how cutting off toxic family relationships is becoming part of a broader societal shift towards healthier personal dynamics, free from guilt. The aim is to destigmatize estrangement and empower individuals to step away from damaging familial interactions without remorse.

Recent statistics underscore the relevance of this issue: according to sociologist Karl Pillemer, 27% of Americans report being estranged from a family member. This figure is significant, highlighting a shift in how we value and maintain family connections. Moreover, Pillemer found that financial disputes and inheritance issues are frequently at the heart of these estrangements.

As the incidence of family estrangement rises, its impact on estate planning becomes more pronounced. These dynamics often compel individuals to make challenging decisions about who will manage their affairs after they're gone. Some may use their Will as a tool for posthumous messages or retribution, while others face the practical challenge of finding someone both willing and capable of taking on the role of executor.

Estrangement and complex family dynamics might necessitate choosing an impartial executor. This decision is vital for those who doubt their family's ability to manage their estate impartially or effectively, possibly due to issues like substance abuse or severed ties.

Take, for instance, my client Walter. Estranged from his

ex-wife and daughter, who completely cut off contact with him, Walter found himself without a trusted family member to oversee his estate. His decision to seek an external executor was driven not by anger or a desire for retribution but by necessity—the simple lack of alternatives. Despite not knowing the intricate details of their fallout, I deeply understood Walter's isolation during a time when most rely heavily on family support.

Walter's choice to interview a bank to act as his executor is a practical solution for those in similar situations. Opting for a professional executor or fiduciary is often the most straightforward way to ensure the estate is managed efficiently and impartially, avoiding additional familial tension.

His situation serves as a poignant reminder of the emotional complexities involved in estate planning. It highlights the importance of tackling these issues directly, striving for reconciliation when possible, or finding alternative solutions that suit one's current family dynamics.

If you find yourself in a position like Walter's, it's wise to consult with a professional who can provide tailored advice. Make sure that your estate plan, including the selection of an executor, accurately reflects your personal wishes and the realities of your family relationships. This approach can help mitigate the emotional and administrative challenges that often arise in the context of estranged family relationships.

I want to emphasize that I have not personally crafted a Will while grappling with the complexities of strained family relationships or other challenging circumstances that necessitate tough decisions about a family member's inheritance.

For example, a relative might struggle with substance abuse, gambling problems, or reckless spending habits, and leaving them a substantial sum might only exacerbate these issues. Nonetheless, I am acquainted with the difficulties of enforcing a Will that includes punitive terms. From my experience, this can place the executor in an extremely challenging position and may turn the estate settlement process from a moment of closure into a contentious battleground. However, I recognize that sometimes individuals are left with no choice but to impose conditional terms or exclude certain beneficiaries entirely to protect the estate and its intentions.

If you are considering conditional terms in your Will due to estrangement or other personal grievances, it is crucial to consult with estate planning experts. These professionals can help navigate these emotionally charged decisions thoughtfully—an approach that I'm sure is self-evident to anyone navigating these difficult waters. Estrangement can significantly complicate estate planning. It's essential to approach these situations with a clear understanding of both the legal implications and the emotional weight they carry. Opting for a professional executor can alleviate some of the burdens and ensure that your estate is settled without unnecessary or additional conflict.

My main point is that regardless of the reasons or circumstances that lead you to include conditional terms in your Will, it is imperative to ensure that your executor is fully aware of the terms they will be enforcing. They must be prepared for the job and any potential friction that may arise. Communication is always key, and being clear is being kind, especially when it comes to defining an executor's responsibilities.

———— ♦ ————

WRAPPING IT UP— A CALL TO ACTION

As we close this chapter on the pitfalls to avoid when appointing an executor, remember that the choices you make today will echo through your family's future. The responsibility of executing an estate is not just about following through on technicalities but also about carrying forward a legacy with respect and care.

Choose Wisely, Plan Thoughtfully

Selecting an executor is more than just ticking a box in your estate planning checklist—it's about entrusting someone with your final wishes and ensuring they have the capacity and integrity to handle the task. It's not a role for the faint-hearted or for those with a packed schedule who might find the duties overwhelming.

The Clear Path Forward

To set your chosen executor up for success:

- **Communicate** Make sure they know they're chosen, understand their duties, and are prepared for the role.
- **Organize** Streamline their job by keeping your documents orderly, your list of assets and debts clear, and your instructions straightforward.
- **Support** Let them know that they should absolutely leverage professional help. First and foremost, an experienced trust and estate attorney, but also an accountant, your financial advisor, and/or an after loss professional to help streamline all aspects of administration.

Legacy of Harmony

Avoid leaving behind a legacy of conflict and chaos. By clearly articulating your wishes, appointing the right person for the job, and ensuring they have what they need to succeed, you can minimize the stress on your loved ones during an already difficult time.

In essence, don't just plan for the end—plan for what happens after. Your thoughtful preparation today can be one of the greatest gifts you leave behind, paving the way for a smooth transition and preserving family harmony. Let's make sure that the role of an executor is a duty of honor rather than a burden of confusion.

So, take a moment today to review your estate plan with these points in mind. It's not just about avoiding the "don'ts" but about embracing the "dos" that make for a truly effective and compassionate conclusion to your life's story.

CHAPTER 09
YOUR ACTIONABLE NEXT STEP: DON'T BE LATE TO YOUR OWN FUNERAL

My mother turned tardiness into an art form. Whether it was collecting us from school last or making a grand entrance as some function was ending, she was never one for punctuality. We'd often joke she'd even be late to her own funeral, and as it turned out, we ensured she was.

My mom's funeral might have been the first in the history of the local funeral home to feature a carefully choreographed run of show. Alongside a lineup that mixed roasts with remembrances, the program included a family tradition—a recitation of Alfred Lord Tennyson's "Crossing the Bar," which had everyone dabbing their eyes—either from tears or stifled laughter from a story that had been shared. The fun photo slideshow, paired with the commanding sound of a Scottish piper, perfectly captured the essence of my mom's funeral, blending tradition with her distinctive flair for quirkiness and humor.

True to form—and with a hint of her timeless humor—I had arranged with the funeral director, Sean, to bring out my mom's urn 30 minutes late. It was our way of letting her be late to her own funeral, literally.

This anecdote isn't just about honoring my mother's quirky habit; it's a metaphor spun into the fabric of this book: **Don't be late to your own funeral.** Throughout these chapters, I've emphasized that timely and thoughtful estate planning is crucial—not just a legal formality but a profound act of consideration for those we leave behind. Delaying or over-simplifying this process can leave a mess as memorable as arriving late to your own final party.

Of course, in my mother's case, her literal tardiness to her funeral was by design—a playful nod to a lifetime of moments. It serves as a gentle reminder: while you can't be late to your own funeral unless you (or your family) plan it that way, you certainly can and should be punctual in planning for it. After all, estate planning is not about hurrying through life; it's about setting the pace for a legacy that endures without the logistical nightmares.

With this in mind, let's pivot from personal anecdotes to practical advice. Here are the indispensable steps and strategies we've discussed, serving as a guide to ensure your estate planning is as structured and deliberate as possible:

PHASE 1:

TAKE INVENTORY, CHECK YOUR GEAR, AND PICK YOUR TEAM

Setting Your Estate Planning Goals

Start with the end in mind. What do you want to achieve with your estate plan? Define your goals clearly to guide the planning process.

List Everything but the Kitchen Sink

- **Assets Galore** Whip out your ledger, virtual or real, and start tallying everything from your castle (or cozy condo) to your coin collection. Remember, if it's worth counting, it counts. Include items such as:
  - Real estate property
  - Vehicles, boats, etc
  - Jewelry, collectibles, and personal possessions
  - Checking and savings accounts
  - Life insurance
  - Retirement accounts
  - Businesses
  - Stocks and bonds
- **Debt Roundup** Line up those debts, including mortgages, loans, and credit card balances. Knowing what you owe is just as crucial as knowing what you own.
  - Credit cards
  - Mortgages
  - Lines of credit
  - Auto loans
  - Any other debts you owe
- **Choose Your Tools** Opt for the most convenient

method to keep track and organized, whether it's a digital spreadsheet or dedicated financial software. Remember to back up your data to safeguard against technological snafus.

Audit Your Estate Planning Docs Like a Pro

- **Gather the Scrolls** If applicable, dig out every piece of legal parchment you've got—Wills, Trusts, financial Power of Attorney, and those fancy advance healthcare directives that say who gets to pull the plug.
- **Needs Assessment** Life changes—marriages, divorces, births, and deaths can all affect your estate planning needs. Make sure your documents reflect your current life circumstances.

Organize the Paper Trail

- **Essential Papers** Where's the deed to the house? Titles to your cars? Ensure all documents (i.e., deeds, titles, birth certificates, Social Security cards) and information are available and organized so your family doesn't have to turn into amateur detectives when the time comes.
- **Secure the Fort** Consider getting a fireproof safe over a bank's safe deposit box. You want your heirs to access these without having to crack a vault in the case that they weren't given authorized access at the bank ahead of time and/or if they don't have the keys.

Choose Your A Team

- **Guardian Angel** Got kids? Pick someone who can actually keep up with them. Confirm they're up for the gig—nobody likes unexpected babysitting duty.

- **Pet Protector** Who's going to inherit the noble duty of feeding Mittens the cat? Maybe set aside a kitty fund to cover those gourmet tuna treats.
- **Executor or Trustee** Choose wisely—no co-executors. This isn't a buddy cop movie; you need one good hero. Don't forget about naming a backup.
- **Power Players** Appoint a financial guru as your Power of Attorney and an aging-savvy advocate for medical decisions. These folks need to be clear-headed and ready to step up, not just warm bodies.

By following these steps in Phase 1, you lay a strong foundation for your estate plan, ensuring that all aspects of your life are accounted for and managed according to your wishes.

PHASE 2:
THINK GLOBALLY, ACT LOCALLY

Plan Beyond Just Documents

Estate planning transcends mere paperwork; it's about capturing the essence of your life and how you want to be remembered. This involves more than asset distribution—it's about honoring your personal values and leaving a lasting impact.

Define Your Legacy Goals
- What do you want to be remembered for?
- How do you want your personal values and life experiences reflected in your legacy?
- Example: If you've been a lifelong supporter of the arts, consider setting up a scholarship for local students in the arts.

Document Cultural and Family Traditions
- List and describe important family and cultural tra-

ditions that you want to be preserved or honored.
- Consider creating a family heritage book or video that can be passed down to future generations.
- Whether it's annual family gatherings, secret recipes, or personal rituals, ensure these are well noted for future generations.

Personal Care Decisions
- Detail your preferences for scenarios in which you cannot communicate your wishes, including specifics on palliative care and any medical interventions you would prefer to avoid.
- Outline your preferences for medical care in scenarios where you can't make decisions yourself. From life support choices to organ donation preferences, these directives ensure your health care aligns with your personal values.

Aging in Place Preferences
- Whether it's retiring in a community like Shady Pines with farm-to-table dining or staying in your longtime home, your plan should reflect your preferences while also weighing the pros and cons of both.
- Evaluate the feasibility of aging in place by considering modifications your home may need to accommodate health changes.
- Explore community resources or services that support aging in place.

End-of-Life Preferences
- Reflecting on what matters most to you at the end of life is essential for guiding your care decisions. Consider what's most important to you, such as "maintaining my independence for as long as possible" or "ensuring I can spend my final days at home surrounded by family."

- Discuss and document your preferred setting for the end of life—whether it's at home, in a hospice, or another comforting environment—and specify who you would like to have by your side.
- Consider the atmosphere you'd want at the end of life. For instance, my mom always said she wanted Tchaikovsky's "1812 Overture" playing on her deathbed so she could go out with a bang!

Funeral or Memorial Preferences
- **Lasting Impressions** Choosing how to exit the stage of life is no small decision. Make sure your preference is known, whether it's a traditional burial at the old family plot, cremation, or a more contemporary choice like a green burial or aquamation—no, it's not the latest thrill ride at a Canadian waterpark, but a gentler, more eco-friendly way to say goodbye using water. It's kind of like being environmentally conscious, even posthumously.
- **Setting the Tone** What's the soundtrack of your life? Whether it's Frank Sinatra's "My Way," David Bowie's "Starman," or something a little more serene like "Somewhere Over the Rainbow," choose music that sets the right mood at your memorial. This isn't just background noise; it's the playlist of your final party.
- **Personal Touches** Specify any rituals or ceremonies you want featured. From a Viking funeral (longboat not included) to a simple candlelight vigil, it's your scene, so direct it as you wish.
- **Your Life in Words** Fancy writing your own obituary? It's your chance to tell your story your way—no embellishments necessary. Plus, it's one less job for your busy relatives, and you ensure no one forgets that award you won in third grade.

Don't Overlook the Digital

Rethinking Password Lists

Keeping a written list of passwords might seem straight-forward, but it's actually a snapshot that quickly becomes outdated. Financial advisors, attorneys, and other estate planning experts sometimes suggest recording this information for executors or trustees. However, this approach has a fundamental flaw: passwords change. Furthermore, while sharing passwords might feel harmless—it's actually against most terms of service agreements. Many companies are shifting towards passkeys, which allow users to authenticate and log in without having to enter a username or password. Whether due to security policies, forgotten passwords, or routine updates, the digital keys to our online lives evolve frequently, rendering any written list potentially obsolete and inaccurate.

Instead of relying on a static list, consider using a password manager. These tools not only store passwords securely but also make updates and management straightforward without compromising security.

A Better Strategy

- **Expand Your Inventory** When you create a comprehensive inventory of your estate—which includes everything from real estate and bank accounts to personal items and investments—make sure to integrate your digital assets into the same system. Think broader than social media—including email accounts, subscription services, digital storage, and more. Create and secure a list of the following:
  - ◉ Email Accounts
  - ◉ Messaging Services
  - ◉ Social Media

⊙ Payment/Money Management
⊙ Electronic Devices
⊙ Household or Property Accounts
⊙ Shopping and Video Accounts
⊙ Loyalty, Reward, and Frequent Flyer Accounts
⊙ Cloud Storage Repositories
⊙ Business Interests: URLs, trademarks, software, videos, logos, slide decks, spreadsheets

- **Use Online Planning Tools** As we mentioned in Chapter 5, utilize tools like Facebook's Memorialization Settings, Apple's Legacy Contact, and Google's Inactive Account Manager to ensure your digital assets are managed according to your wishes after your death.
- **Keep Records Updated** Ensure all your digital account details are current, complete, and stored securely.
- **Secure Storage Solutions** Document where your digital assets are and how they can be accessed. Opt for secure solutions such as password managers or digital vaults to organize and protect access details. These tools keep your digital estate well-ordered and easily transferable to your executor or trustee.
- **Sharing is Caring** Make sure your executor or trusted contact has the unlock code and password for your phone and computer, laptop, or other device.

I know this has been quite a journey through Phase 2, setting the stage with detailed, thoughtful planning. By embracing this holistic approach to estate planning, you've paved the way for a smoother transition into Phase 3.

PHASE 3:
LEGALLY LOCK IT DOWN

Congratulations, you've reached the legal stage, also known as the "make it official" phase! You've done the heavy lifting by sorting your assets and dreams; now, it's time to make sure they stick, legally speaking.

Selecting the Right Legal Help
Time to find your legal eagle! Picking the right attorney isn't like grabbing a coffee; you need someone who knows their Trusts from their estates. Here's how to spot the attorney who can navigate the murky waters of estate law:

- **Experience** "What is your experience with trust and estate law?"
- **Timeline** "How long will it take to complete my estate plan?"
- **Communication** "What will be the best way to communicate with you?"
- **Fees** "Can you break down your fees?"
- **Education-first** "Can you help me understand the pros and cons of the estate planning documents and strategy you're recommending?"

Budgeting for the Legal Lockdown
I totally get that estate planning feels like a huge chore. It's not just a time-eater; it gobbles up your hard-earned cash, too. And to put it plainly, in times when every penny counts, shelling out for legal fees might seem like the last thing you want to do.

The cost of drafting a Will with an attorney can really vary. You might get away with spending less than a thousand bucks for the straightforward stuff, but if your estate is more like a season of *Succession*—think businesses, multiple properties, or a big family—then brace yourself. Costs could zoom to anywhere between $7,000 and $10,000, according to CNBC. Why such a leap?

First off, it's all about how complicated your situation is. If you're juggling a business, a bunch of properties, or a large family, things get intricate pretty fast. For instance, if you're a business owner, you've got to figure out what happens to your slice of the pie when you're no longer around.

Then there's the asset list—yeah, rounding up everything you own and deciding who receives what can be a mammoth task. And if you're feeling generous toward your favorite charities, planning those donations adds another layer to the Will.

And don't forget that the attorney's experience level and where you live can play a big part, too. Costs can vary just because of your zip code, what lawyers around there tend to charge, and how many years they've been practicing in the trust and estate realm.

So, keeping all these things in mind can help you navigate the cost of getting your Will done without too many surprises. Finding the right attorney for your estate planning isn't just about who's available—it's about finding a perfect match for your needs, goals, and budget. Here's how to make sure you get the best bang for your buck without compromising on quality:

- **Shop Around** Interview at least three to compare their expertise, demeanor, and pricing.
- **Discovery Calls** Many attorneys offer a free initial consultation, often about 30 minutes. Use this time wisely to gauge their understanding of your specific needs and to see if they're a good personal fit.
- **Match Your Needs** If you have unique circumstances like business ownership or out-of-state properties, you'll need someone experienced in handling such complexities.
- **Personality Fit** Since this is someone you'll need to discuss personal and potentially sensitive details with, it's crucial that you feel comfortable and trust them.
- **Budget Alignment** A good attorney will be upfront about whether they can work within your financial parameters or not.
- **Check References** Ask for references from past clients with similar estate planning needs.

But fear not! There are some wallet-friendly moves you can make today, even amidst the budget squeeze:

- **List It Out** I know I've said it 100 times in this book, but I'll say it again for posterity. Make a comprehensive list of what you own and what you owe. This is step one in any estate plan and costs nothing but a bit of your time.
- **Direct Designations** Look into Payable on Death (POD) arrangements for bank accounts or Transfer on Death (TOD) stipulations for brokerage accounts. This way, you keep control over your assets while alive, but they pass directly to your named beneficiary upon death, bypassing the probate process.
- **Beneficiary Benefits** Don't forget about naming

beneficiaries directly on policies like life insurance, pensions, or retirement accounts (like IRAs or 401(k)s). These can pass outside of probate and are pretty straightforward to set up.
- **Leverage Online Planning Tools** As we mentioned in Phase 2, incorporate services like Apple's Legacy Contact, Facebook's Memorialization Settings, and Google's Inactive Account Manager into your plan. These tools help ensure that your digital assets are accessible and not locked away upon your incapacity or death. Think of these tools as the digital age's answer to beneficiary designations.

Creating and Finalizing Essential Documents
With the perfect attorney on board, it's time to get drafting:

- **Financial Power of Attorney** This indispensable document assigns a trusted individual to manage your finances should you become unable to do so yourself. From making sure your bills are paid to keeping your investments on track, this person will ensure your financial affairs continue to hum along smoothly.
- **Advance Healthcare Directives and Medical Power of Attorney** Just as vital, these documents ensure that someone you trust can oversee your healthcare decisions if you're not able to make them yourself. Advance healthcare directives specify your preferences for medical care, detailing which treatments you would or would not want to receive, thereby guiding your healthcare even when you can't voice your decisions. A medical power of attorney goes hand-in-hand, authorizing a specific individual to make healthcare decisions that adhere to your established preferences, covering decisions from everyday treatment options

to critical medical actions.

- **Last Will and Testament and/or Trust** Crucial moments like these call for either drafting a new or updating an existing Will or Trust. These documents detail the distribution of your assets, ensuring they pass on according to your wishes. It's also essential to align and update any designated beneficiaries on life insurance policies and retirement accounts to avoid discrepancies and ensure they reflect your current intentions.

- **Comprehensive Authority** Ensure all documents clearly empower your agent, executor, or trustee to manage both your digital and tangible assets. Embed precise language that gives them the authority to handle and distribute your digital possessions just as effectively as they would your physical ones. This clarity in your legal documents will help prevent any ambiguity or legal hurdles down the road, ensuring a smoother transition of all your assets.

Ensuring Access to Funds

Ensure your executor has immediate access to funds to handle initial expenses. Make sure to talk this through with your attorney so that you don't contradict your estate plan, but some options include:

- Allocating a life insurance policy to cover immediate costs (like funeral expenses) can provide significant financial relief.
- Setting up a dedicated savings account with easy executor access.
- Designating accounts as Payable on Death (POD) or Transfer on Death (TOD) to facilitate quick transfer to beneficiaries without probate.

Executor Etiquette: Setting Them Up for Success
- **Choose Your Executor, Agent, and/Or Trustee Wisely** Picking the right executor is critical. Make sure you have the right executor for the job, and make sure your executor knows how to access the information they need. It's tempting to name more than one to balance the responsibility, but this often leads to more complications than it solves. A single, reliable executor tends to be more effective, preventing potential conflicts and ensuring the estate is settled efficiently.
- **Maintain Clear Communication** Regular updates with beneficiaries prevent misunderstandings and disputes, ensuring everyone understands your estate planning intentions.

Safeguarding Your Documents
Once your newly executed or updated estate planning docs are signed, sealed, and delivered, make sure you think through where you keep your Will and other important documents, as it can affect how easily your estate is settled.

- Choose a secure, accessible location for your Will—like a fireproof safe in your home, which avoids the complications of retrieving it from a bank safety deposit box.
- Digital backups can be invaluable, especially considering possible natural disasters. Using secure cloud storage services to keep copies of important documents ensures they survive any physical damage to your home.
- Document Accessibility: Clearly communicate the location of your Will and other estate documents to your executor and key family members to prevent a frantic search.

Update, Update, Update Change is the only constant. Update your estate plan as routinely as spring cleaning, but hopefully, it will be less dusty. Keep your documents as current as your social media profiles, ensuring they reflect the latest plot twists in your family saga.

By treating estate planning as a regular item on your family's agenda, you turn potential chaos into a well-organized plan. This way, you're not just passing on assets but also peace of mind, wrapped up in a plan that's as neat as your freshly organized sock drawer.

Mind the "5 D's" from the American Bar Association's Commission on Law and Aging as triggers for reviewing and updating your estate plan:

- Death of a family member or friend
- Divorce
- Diagnosis of a new medical condition
- Decline in health
- Arrival of a new decade in your life

———— ⚰ ————

PHASE 4:
KEEP 'EM IN THE LOOP

After neatly organizing everything from assets to healthcare directives in the earlier phases, it's time for Phase 4. This is more than just a casual coffee chat; it's the crucial phase where you make sure your carefully laid plans don't evaporate into a family mystery after you're gone.

Host a Family Pow-Wow Imagine trying to follow a recipe written in invisible ink. That's your family without a clear rundown of your estate plan. Schedule a family or executor meeting to lay it all out. Think of it as a "show and tell" but with less glitter and more deeds and directives.

Pulling off a family meeting about estate planning doesn't have to be as stiff as a boardroom session. Here's how to keep it relaxed yet effective:

- **Give Everyone a Heads Up** Loop in everyone early. Find a time that works for all, even if it means some folks need to dial in for a video chat.
- **Pick a Comfy Spot** Choose a place where everyone feels at ease, ensuring privacy and comfort, especially for the person whose estate plan is on the table. Serving drinks and snacks might be good to keep everyone's blood sugar and mood on the up and up.
- **Choose a Ring Leader** Appoint someone to keep the chat on track. They're not the boss but more like a meeting referee.
- **Lay Out the Plan** Make sure everyone knows what's up for discussion—Wills, Trusts, who gets to be the executor, and all that important stuff. This helps keep the chat focused.
- **Collect the Docs** Round up all necessary paperwork beforehand, like current Wills or financial statements. Don't forget about the digital stuff, too.

By transforming estate planning into an ongoing family dialogue, you turn potential chaos into a coherent plan. This proactive approach doesn't just pass on assets; it hands down a legacy of clarity and peace, ensuring your loved ones are well-prepared to manage without you, with all the instructions they need neatly packed like your meticulously organized sock drawer.

——— 🪦 ———

LET'S TALK ABOUT DEATH, BABY: NAVIGATING THE "D" WORD WITH FAMILY

Now, what about when the tables are turned? When it's your turn to steer the conversation about estate planning with your aging parents or other relatives, it can feel as absurd as persuading a cat to joyfully jump into a bubble bath.

It's a common struggle. I often hear clients and friends say, "My parents won't even discuss this," or "Every time I bring it up, the conversation just shuts down." Or even more daunting, "My mom starts crying and asks if I'm waiting for her to die every time I mention it." Yep, that's a conversation stopper.

Still, it's crucial, especially when the usual response to the topic is, "Can we change the subject?" Here's how to gently crack open that dialogue without causing a dinner table revolt.

Ice Breakers That Won't Freeze the Room

- **Help Wanted** "I need your help with something that's really important. Yes, more important than watching the kids while we go to Cabo next month."
- **Tell Tall Tales** Use stories of estate disasters as a non-threatening way to show what could go wrong. "You know how Uncle Bob's circus of an estate went down? Let's avoid that circus tent, shall we?"
- **Look Ahead** "Let's make a pact to avoid any future family drama over who gets the antique spoon collection, okay?"

- **Preemptive Strike** "While everything's good now, I want to keep it that way. Can we talk about a game plan?"
- **Gamify the Grim** Bring in books, card games, or articles that make planning feel less like a chore and more like a trivia night.
- **Holiday Heart-to-Hearts** Turn holiday gatherings into treasure troves of family history and future planning. It's easier to talk about legacies when you're already down memory lane. It's like sneaking veggies into a smoothie—good for them, but easier to swallow.

Rolling with the Questions: Your Estate Planning Conversation Starter Kit

Once you've got everyone to the table, here's your essential list of questions to keep the conversation flowing:

- When was the last time you updated your Will, financial power of attorney, or healthcare directive?
- Where are all important documents kept?
- Do you have a list of your current assets and liabilities?
- What banks and institutions hold your accounts?
- How do you feel about managing the upkeep of your current home?
- What are your thoughts on decluttering and getting rid of some belongings?
- When the time comes, how can immediate expenses be managed?
- How is your digital footprint managed, including passwords and online accounts?
- Have you set up any online planning tools for digital assets, like Apple's Legacy Contact or Google's Inactive Account Manager?
- Does anyone have access to your phone and computer?

Let's be real—kicking off these talks can be as awkward as explaining why you're late to a meeting when you were really just scrolling through social media. And yes, even as a pro, I find these chats challenging! But taking that first step is crucial. Once you start, it paves the way for easier, more open dialogues in the future.

These conversations are best had regularly, not just when a crisis hits. By addressing these topics proactively, you'll turn potential "uh-ohs" into "ahas", easing future transitions. Keep the dialogue alive; it's not just about making the conversation less uncomfortable—it's about crafting peace of mind for everyone involved.

Another tool in your toolbox: The Dinner Party Analogy
If you're still hitting a snag in starting the conversation or are looking for a different angle, one engaging strategy I often use, especially in group presentations, is the Dinner Party Analogy.

Here's the gist: Imagine you're planning a dinner party, a familiar scenario for anyone who's ever played the gracious host. The checklist is extensive: set the date, invite the guests, plan the menu, shop for groceries, prepare the meal, and clean the house, all before the first doorbell rings. Once the party kicks off, you're juggling hosting duties with serving and, eventually, the inevitable cleanup.

But what if you flipped the script? Picture calling your guests with a slight tweak to the plan: "Hey, I'm not up for cooking. Could you whip up something delicious and bring it over?" That's a little cheeky, right?

Now, push that boundary further. Imagine asking them to drop by early—not for pre-party cocktails, but to scrub and sanitize your home from top to bottom. And just when you think you've asked enough of them, you throw in one final request: "After you've enjoyed the dinner you cooked in the house you cleaned, could you also handle the entire clean-up? That'd be Gucci. Thanks!"

It's absurd, right? You're probably cringing at the thought. This is not how gracious hosting works; it's a quick way to ensure your next party is a party of one.

This scenario mirrors life-and-death discussions. Just as it's unreasonable to expect your guests to prep, host, and clean without prior arrangement, it's equally unrealistic—and unfair—to leave your loved ones to sort out your estate without clear instructions. By comparing estate planning to organizing a dinner party, you highlight the importance of preparation and the courtesy of not leaving a mess for others to clean up.

This analogy can lighten the mood and help illustrate the importance of discussing and organizing one's end-of-life plans. It's your party—plan it well so that when it's over, your loved ones aren't left with the burden of cleaning up. After all, a thoughtful host makes all arrangements to ensure their guests leave with nothing but fond memories.

Climbing Over Conversation Hurdles

- **Drop Them A Line** Can't get a word in edgewise? Try writing a letter—it's thoughtful, and hey, they can't interrupt a piece of paper.

- **Book Drop** Leave a helpful book on their coffee table. It's less pushy than a PowerPoint presentation.
- **Persistence Pays Off** Keep at it, but gently. Remember, you're in a marathon, not a sprint.
- **Call in the Cavalry** Sometimes, it's easier to hear it from someone else. Enlist a trusted friend or professional to help make your case.

Remember that patience is key, especially since the topic can touch on sensitive areas. It's best to keep the atmosphere light and pressure-free, akin to a tea party rather than a courtroom setting. Active listening is crucial; allow family members to express their concerns and thoughts first. Staying curious and asking open-ended questions can lead to more comprehensive planning. Remember to jot down important points during these discussions—you'll appreciate having these notes later. Lastly, maintaining an open-door policy by keeping all family members informed can help avoid surprises and ensure everyone is on the same page.

By peppering in a bit of humor and maintaining a light touch, you'll find that these discussions might just become a new family tradition. After all, who said planning for the future had to be all doom and gloom?

Wrapping Us Up

As we wrap up this chapter, remember that estate planning is much like writing the last chapter of your own story. It's about ensuring that the tales, trials, and triumphs of your life are neatly penned, your intentions clearly communicated, and your legacy thoughtfully preserved. It's not merely a task for the here and now but a gift of peace and clarity to those you love, ensuring they aren't left to decipher a puzzle in your absence. So take these steps, engage in those tough conversations, and keep your plan updated. By doing so, you're not just preparing for the inevitable; you're actively caring for your loved ones' future comfort and security. Don't just be remembered fondly—leave behind a blueprint that helps those you cherish navigate forward with confidence and grace.

CHAPTER 10
THE LAST CHAPTER

First off, hats off to you for not tossing this book into a corner where it could gather dust and bitter resentment. I know I've regaled you with story after story of Grade-A flaming dumpster fires, so it's perfectly normal if you're ready to crawl back into bed and pull the covers over your head. Seriously, if you're feeling like you're about to spiral into an existential crisis at the thought of just getting started, you're not alone.

——— 🪦 ———

THE OVERWHELM IS REAL

Now, let's have a real chat. The path to getting your affairs in order isn't just about wading through legal terms, making endless decisions, or filling out a stack of forms—it's also an emotional marathon. Yes, the overwhelm is real, and it's perfectly natural to feel swamped by the sheer scale of what lies ahead. However, thinking you can tackle all of this in one go is like trying to eat a whale in one bite—it's not just impossible, it's ridiculous.

But here's the silver lining: **you don't have to do it all or all at once.** Even if you take some or any of the advice I've outlined in this book, you will be far better off than most Americans who have no estate planning whatsoever.

I know I've overloaded you with homework in this book, which you may not have time to be able to or want to complete. Even if this avalanche of information makes you want to hit the snooze button indefinitely, there are simple steps you can take now to transform your overwhelmed sighs into triumphant "ahas." By following the actionable steps laid out in this book, you'll find it surprisingly doable to leave ease instead of anguish for your family.

Dip back into Chapter 9, pick any section that resonates with you, and start there. Remember, you're not solving global crises—just preventing a personal one for your loved ones.

Listen, if you or a family member is one of those people who just can't be convinced that this is worth the time, effort, or cost, or they're one of those die-hard "Why do I care? I'll be dead types," here's the bare minimum of estate planning in my humble opinion.

For the "I'll Be Dead Anyway" Brigade: The Bare Minimum Estate Planning Guide

For those who think this effort isn't worth the time or expense or who are sticking to their guns on their "I'll be dead anyway" mantra, here's what I think is the absolute least you should do:

- **Will you tell me already?** Simply letting someone know you haven't or don't plan to make a Will is both crucial and considerate. It prevents a futile search for something that doesn't exist. Remember, though, that without a Will, state laws dictate what happens to your estate, which might not reflect your wishes.
- **Prepping for the Unthinkable** More than anything, I'm concerned about what happens if you're incapacitated. Navigating care for someone who can't express their wishes is tough and costly. Set up advance directives like a living Will and a durable power of attorney for healthcare to outline your medical preferences. Free advance directive forms are available from reliable sources such as AARP at aarp.org.
- **Beneficiary Basics** Prioritize naming beneficiaries on all your financial accounts. This simple step ensures that assets like bank accounts, retirement funds, and life insurance policies pass directly to your chosen beneficiaries. It's the easiest way to ensure your assets go exactly where you want them with the least amount of fuss.
- **Digital Keys to the Kingdom** Don't overlook your digital legacy. Utilize the tools we referenced in the last chapter to manage your digital assets according to your wishes after your death. Also, share your digital access codes—like your phone's unlock code and computer password. This basic step ensures your family or trusted contact can access important information, from photos to what banking apps you have, at least starting them on the right path.

——— ⚰ ———

NOT EVERY STORY IS A DEBBIE DOWNER

For every face-palm moment and story of estate misman-
agement I've shared, let's balance the scales with some tales
where things went right. Yes, it's true! While I admit portions
of this book seem about as uplifting as *Angela's Ashes*, estate
planning can sometimes work out beautifully, turning gridlock into a couple of mere traffic lights.

Navigating Probate with Precision

Consider my client Harrison, who was taken off guard after
his father died unexpectedly. Despite not having any warn-
ing, Harrison's family didn't descend into chaos, thanks to
his dad's obsession with detail. Their probate journey was
less of a horror story, and more of a masterclass in meticu-
lousness, with every property and penny accounted for in a
Trust that cleverly skipped over the usual probate hurdles.
This wasn't just legal prowess; it was a family bonding activ-
ity, uniting them in grief but not in legal gridlock, allowing
them to pass Go, collect their emotional bearings, and focus
on celebrating a life well-lived.

Philanthropy Through Planning

Meet Rhonda and Dave, a couple who are very involved and
active in their small town. Not content with merely attending every community fundraiser, they turned their estate
plan into a work of art. By setting up a charitable Trust, they
ensured their passion for the arts would play on like a timeless symphony, providing scholarships for aspiring artists.
This savvy move helped to keep their tax liability lower and

their community spirits high, painting their legacy across the canvas of their beloved town.

A Strategy for Serenity

And then there's Sam, whose story highlights the practical benefits of documenting what was most important to him at the end of his life. Sam got ahead of the game by mapping out his end-of-life wishes early on. He put everything in black and white—no resuscitation, yes to dying at home, and all while Debussy's "Clair de Lune" played in the background. He even asked that his friends and family tell their favorite stories of their time together at his bedside.

When the time came, this foresight paid off big time. His family wasn't stuck making tough calls during tough times, and there were no fiery disputes to extinguish. Instead, Sam got his wish: to be at home, surrounded by family stories and the familiar strains of his favorite tune, making his final days as peaceful as planned. His story is a nudge for everyone: clear plans make things a heck of a lot easier for everyone involved. It's about letting your loved ones focus on being together, not on fretting over decisions.

So, you see, there are times when planning ahead can help things go as planned. Did everything go perfectly? No. Did it require uncomfortable, perfunctory planning ahead? Yes. And most importantly, despite all that was done ahead of time, was it still hard as hell to navigate the loss of someone who was loved so dearly? Yes.

These stories illuminate the brighter side of estate planning, where so much can go right when things are done right. And I wish like heck that there were more stories like them.

I always think back to something my friend, author, and fellow deathcare industry colleague Jennifer O'Brien always says: "There are no do-overs in end-of-life." So, while we can't control everything, detailed planning can certainly smooth out many bumps along the way.

—— 🪦 ——

MAN, I WISH THINGS HAD BEEN DIFFERENT, BUT BOY, I HAVE LEARNED A LOT

I can see that it wasn't always easy, especially when it came to dealing with death. I was introduced to life's hard lessons too early and too often. The jury is still out on whether or not it's serendipity or quite the opposite. I'll let you know if I figure it out. I've been handed quite a few lemons in life, yet here I am, making lemonade. And let me tell you, it's both tart and transformative.

Death has seemed to have a VIP pass to my life's events, show-ing up uninvited and often. Navigating through those times was often a Herculean task. Was I still extremely fortunate? Absolutely. I had two parents who loved me unconditionally, provided for me, taught me independence, showed me how to view life through a different lens, the value of hard work, and how to be resourceful as hell.

Yet, here's the twist—through my uphill battles, I found my calling. It's strange to say, but each of those gut-wrenching goodbyes taught me something invaluable. I learned the ropes of estate planning, probate navigation, and how to really listen to those grappling with grief. It was a master-class in the messiness of mortality, taught by life itself.

Now, I've turned those lessons into a lifeline for others. It's weirdly wonderful to take my catalog of calamities and turn it into a guidebook for those lost in the labyrinth of loss. I consider it a privilege, truly. Helping people manage their darkest days and make sense of the senseless isn't just a job—it's a mission. It's about taking the sour, the bitter, and yes, the bureaucratic and mixing it into something that resembles relief or maybe, on a good day, peace.

So, while I wouldn't necessarily wish my path on others, I'm here, shaker in hand, ready to mix up a better experience for those who follow. If life's going to keep throwing lemons, I might as well keep the lemonade flowing—and maybe sometimes I'll spike it with some vodka.

FACING THE INEVITABLE WITH A NEW LENS

While finding my calling in the realm of after loss services hasn't equipped me with a super-secret ninja way to dodge the inevitabilities of life and death, it has shown me that the end is something none of us can escape—no matter how deftly we manage everything else. Accepting this fact isn't just tough; it's often overwhelming. When the weight of this reality begins to bear down, that's my cue to put pencils down, take a breath, and dive into a sea of gratitude. Yes, it's a bit cliché, but acknowledging what's going right really helps reframe my perspective, granting me the strength to navigate another day of post-mortem chaos for my clients. That's my silent prayer, at least.

Death is a constant in my line of work, and while I'm not suggesting you make it a fixture in your daily life, perhaps we could all benefit from peeling back its mystique a bit. Why? Because speaking openly about death demystifies it, making it easier to address when it does inevitably touch our lives.

So how can you do that? Each year, on my birthday, I have a thought. Between contemplating the existential significance of cake and wondering if I can get away with counting only the candles that didn't melt, a thought strikes me: Why do we save our deepest reflections and heartfelt sentiments for funerals when the guest of honor can't even snort-laugh at the punchlines?

Imagine a world where we roast our loved ones with kindness while they're still around to enjoy it. A world where "I love yous" and "She lit up the room" are served up like slices of birthday cake—frequently and with gusto.

Here's how we might change the narrative:

- **Heartfelt Notes** Unleash your inner poet. Capture the essence of your affections as if you were penning a classic—only with less doom and more bloom. Let them know they're the kind of person who makes ordinary days feel like scenes from a blockbuster movie.
- **Reconnect With Laughter** Grab your phone and dial up a friend. Skip the pleasantries and dive straight into the "remember when" moments. It's like your very own time machine, only with more giggles and less quantum physics.

- **Shower People With Compliments** Don't skimp on the accolades. If you think someone's doing a bang-up job, shout it from the rooftops—or maybe just across the dinner table. Turn every day into a chance to make someone's ego swell just a little.

This advice isn't just for my readers; it's a mantra I need to remind myself of constantly. We can never be sure when we'll run out of opportunities to express our feelings. There's often no perfect time, no ideal moment. The best time to share love and gratitude is now—right this second. So go ahead, write that heartfelt note, make that overdue call, and scatter your compliments as if you're leading the most jubilant parade.

Take, for instance, the weekend before my mother's major surgery—a procedure aimed at removing the "Chicago-sized" tumor. I had a girl's trip planned, one that had been on the books for months. The Airbnb was booked under my name, making me feel like there was no way I could bail. Despite knowing the gravity of the surgery and the daunting odds we faced, I went on that trip. To this day, I deeply regret that decision.

I think about the conversations we could have had, the fears and hopes we could have shared. Instead of saving my truest words for her eulogy, I wish I'd had the courage to sit beside her and say something like, "Mom, this is terrifying. I hope with all my heart that you come through this with flying colors. But just in case, I want to make sure there's nothing left unsaid between us."

That missed opportunity has taught me the importance of being present, especially during the times when it feels hardest to do so. It's a stark reminder that planning for the worst and hoping for the best is the most profound gesture of love we can offer.

—— ⚰ ——

EMBRACING EVERY MOMENT—LIVING FULLY UNTIL THE END

This advice isn't just theoretical; it can be deeply personal and urgent. Recently, I attended a special screening of the documentary *A Butterfly Has Been Released,* produced by friends and fellow "deaducators," Jason Zamer and Barry Koch of TG Beyond.

The film shares the poignant story of hospice nurse Allyson during her last thirty-nine days, living with brain cancer. With an openness that's both inspiring and raw, Allyson invited us into her "living funeral," where heartfelt reflections from loved ones and scenes from her natural, green burial were shared.

Allyson lived her final days with authenticity, showing us the profound impact of facing our mortality head-on and continuing to create meaning and legacy up to the very end. Allyson's humor and wisdom remind us that we're not truly gone if we're still speaking, still impacting lives. Her words, "I'm not dead if I'm still talking," resonate as a powerful testament to living life fully, on our own terms.

Just as Allyson demonstrated, funerals can and should celebrate life. This brings us back to the importance of getting our affairs in order. By preparing, you give room for both grieving and celebration rather than becoming a prelude to a daunting list of tasks for your loved ones to untangle. Planning isn't just about staving off chaos—it's about ensuring your legacy is remembered joyously without burdening those you love.

—— 🜚 ——

THE LAST WORD—EMBRACE THE JOURNEY WITH A CHUCKLE

As we tie up the loose ends of this book, let's remember: the road from birth to beyond is as distinct as every quirky anecdote shared between these covers. Through exploring the nuts and bolts of estate planning, we've also dipped our toes into the emotional whirlpools that come with preparing for the final curtain call—laughing, pondering, and, yes, even muttering a curse word or two.

Consider this book more than a manual; think of it as your gentle nudge into those conversations everyone else is avoiding, like the weird carrot on a vegetable tray. It's your invitation to not only prepare for the end but to squeeze every drop out of life with gusto and maybe a little grace.

Let's not wait for the stars to align to express our feelings or get our affairs in order. Life doesn't pause, and neither should we. Dive into those tough talks, make plans for the "just in case," and celebrate the mundane every chance you get. Laugh with abandon, love without reservations, and plan not just for your peace of mind but for the sanity of those you'll eventually leave in charge.

Keep this book within arm's reach—a guide today, a reminder tomorrow. Flip back through as life throws its curveballs, as your world evolves, and as you continue to grow. After all, the finest legacies are crafted from a mix of careful planning, heartfelt connections, and the ability to laugh at the chaos of it all.

In closing, remember: you're not just setting the stage for a grand exit; you're scripting a masterpiece of memories. So, live spiritedly, plan thoughtfully, and leave a legacy that's less of a bureaucratic maze and more of a treasure map sprinkled with hints of joy and whispers of wisdom.

Now, go on—live well, plan smart, and let your legacy be the light that guides the way, not just a list of instructions left in a dusty old drawer. And who knows? Maybe throw a little confetti at your next family meeting—because if life's going to be a party, you might as well make it freaking fabulous.

ENDNOTES

Page 31: " After-Loss Tech Wants to Ease the Logistics of Death." Accessed at https://www.wired.com/story/after-loss-death-tech/.

Page 41: "2025 Wills and Estate Planning Study." Caring.com. Accessed at https://www.caring.com/caregivers/estate-planning/wills-survey/.

Page 59: "Poll Reveals Over 50 Different Euphemisms for Death." Marie Curie. Available from https://www.mariecu-rie.org.uk/media/press-releases/poll-reveals-over-50-differ-ent-euphemisms-for-death/.

Pages 69, 79-81: Sharp, R. (2017). *Living Trusts for Everyone: Why a Will Is Not the Way to Avoid Probate, Protect Heirs, and Settle Estates* (Second Edition). Allworth.

Pages 79-81: Hower, R., & Kahn, P. (2008). *Wills, Trusts, and Estate Administration* (Sixth Edition). Delmar Cengage Learning.

Page 102: "The Last Goodbye: Best New Ways To Plan A Funeral." *Consumer Reports*, August 2024.

Page 107: Hartung, S., & Zegel, J. L. (2022). *Digital Asset Entanglement: Unraveling the Intersection of Estate Laws & Technology*. LexisNexis.

Page 109: "NetChoice-Commissioned Survey." NetChoice. Accessed at https://www.netchoice.org/afterlife/.

Page 113-114: Forbes Advisor. (2024). 6 best password

managers. Forbes. Updated October 30, 2024. Retrieved from https://www.forbes.com/advisor/business/software/best-password-managers/.

Page 119: "The Landscape of Marriage and Cohabitation in the U.S." Pew Research Center. Available from https://www.pewresearch.org/social-trends/2019/11/06/the-landscape-of-marriage-and-cohabitation-in-the-u-s/.

Page 121: "The '5 D's' for Reviewing Clients' Advance Directives." American Academy of Estate Planning Attorneys. Accessed at https://www.aaepa.com/2012/09/5-ds-reviewing-clients-advance-directives/.

Page 150: "Funeral Homes Don't Have to List Prices Online. That May Change." The New York Times. Available from https://www.nytimes.com/2023/04/14/your-money/funeral-homes-prices-online.html/.

Page 150: "Funeral Pricing Transparency May Tip the Scales in Favor of Consumers." North Carolina Health News. Accessed at https://www.northcarolinahealthnews.org/2024/07/13/funeral-home-pricing-transparency-may-tip-the-scales-in-favor-of-consumers/.

Page 152: "Dying Can Cost Loved Ones $20,000 Before Lost Wages and Worse Health, New Report Says." Forbes. Accessed at https://www.forbes.com/sites/debgordon/2023/01/31/dying-can-cost-loved-ones-20000-before-lost-wages-and-worse-health-new-report-says/.

Page 152: "Cost of Dying Report 2024." Empathy. Available from https://www.empathy.com/costofdying/.

Page 153: "What You Can Expect to Pay a Lawyer During Probate." Empathy. Accessed at https://www.empathy.com/probate/what-you-can-expect-to-pay-a-lawyer-during-probate/.

Page 154: "What Are The Best and Worst States to Die In When You Want to Stay Rich?" FastWill. Accessed at https://fastwill.com/estate-planning-guide/estate-planning/the-best-and-worst-states-to-die-in-when-you-want-to-stay-rich/.

Page 155: "Does a Person's Debt Go Away When They Die?" Consumer Financial Protection Bureau. Accessed at https://www.consumerfinance.gov/ask-cfpb/does-a-persons-debt-go-away-when-they-die-en-1463/.

Page 155: "What Happens to Medical Debt When You Die?" Experian. Accessed at https://www.experian.com/blogs/ask-experian/what-happens-to-medical-debt-when-you-die/.

Page 157: "5 Lessons I Learned About Debt After My Dad's Death That Everyone Should Know." *Business Insider*, 2024, www.businessinsider.com/dad-died-massive-medical-debt-2024-8/.

Page 158: "The Costs of Settling an Estate." American Academy of Estate Planning Attorneys. Accessed at https://www.aaepa.com/2014/03/costs-of-settling-the-estate/.

Page 160: "For Employees Settling A Loved One's Affairs, There's Never Enough Time." *Empathy*, https://www.empathy.com/employer-resources/for-employees-settling-a-loved-ones-affairs-theres-never-enough-time/.

Page 160: "Estate Settlement and Executor Statistics." *Estate-*

Exec, www.estateexec.com/Docs/General_Statistics/.

Page 162: "The State of Women and Caregiving." Caregiving. com. Available from https://www.caregiving.com/content/ women-and-caregiving-2021/.

Page 188: "Why So Many People Are Going 'No Contact' with Their Parents." *The New Yorker,* Available from www.newyorker.com/culture/annals-of-inquiry/why-so-many-people-are-going-no-contact-with-their-parents/.

Page 189: "Psychology Today on 'Fault Lines' and Family Estrangement." *Karl Pillemer,* www.karlpillemer.com/ psychology-today-on-fault-lines-and-family-estrangement/.

Page 189: "What Research Tells Us About Family Estrangement." *Psychology Today,* Available from www.psychology-today.com/us/blog/brothers-sisters-strangers/202402/statistics-that-tell-the-story-of-family-estrangement/.

Page 205: "Can't Afford an Estate Plan? Here's What You Can Do Without Spending a Fortune." CNBC. Available from https://www.cnbc.com/2021/01/03/cant-afford-an-estate-plan-what-to-do-without-spending-a-fortune/.

Page 205: "Average Cost of a Will." *Business Insider.* Accessed at https://www.businessinsider.com/personal-finance/ investing/how-much-does-it-cost-to-make-a-will/.

Page 228: Koch, B. & Zamer, J. (Producers). (2024). *A Butterfly Has Been Released* [Film; online video]. TGBeyond.

HELPFUL RESOURCES & TOOLS

Note: These resources and tools are carefully selected to ensure you have access to the best possible support and information for managing estate planning and dealing with after loss challenges.

The use of brand names and/or any mention or listing of specific commercial products or services herein is solely for educational purposes and does not imply endorsement by me nor discrimination against similar brands, products, or services not mentioned.

ADVANCE CARE AND END-OF-LIFE PLANNING

AARP Offers free, state-specific advance directive forms. Learn more at aarp.org.

Compassion & Choices Provides information and advocacy for end-of-life care options. Learn more at compassionandchoices.org.

Five Wishes Helps you articulate and document your end-of-life care preferences clearly. Learn more at fivewishes.org.

Genworth's Cost of Care Survey Tool Helps estimate future care costs, which is crucial for financial planning. Learn more at genworth.com.

Kitchen Table Conversations Offers free End of Life, Advance Care Planning and Grief Education webinars. Learn more at kitchentableconversations.org.

The Conversation Project Encourages family discussions about end-of-life wishes. Learn more at theconversationproject.org.

The Death Deck This game facilitates easier conversations about death in a light-hearted manner. Learn more at thedeathdeck.com.

DOWNSIZING AND MEMORY PRESERVATION

Artifcts From saving memories while decluttering to preserving the value behind your things, Artifcts gives you a digital way to organize stuff and capture the meaning behind objects. Learn more at artifcts.com.

Infinity Trunk A fireproof and waterproof keepsake trunk ideal for keeping family heirlooms and memories safe and organized. Learn more at infinitytrunk.com.

***Keep the Memories, Lose the Stuff: Declutter, Downsize, and Move Forward with Your Life* by Matt Paxton** More than just a decluttering guide; it's a compassionate and humorous approach to downsizing.

LifeBook Create a personal memoir with professional help—preserving your stories for generations. Learn more at lifetimememoirs.com.

***The Gentle Art of Swedish Death Cleaning: How to Free Yourself and Your Family from a Lifetime of Clutter* by Margareta Magnusson** Offers a practical approach to downsizing that helps you streamline your possessions meaningfully.

The Photo Managers A network of experts dedicated to helping you curate and celebrate your photographic memories. For more details on their services, visit thephotomanagers.com.

FINDING A TRUST AND ESTATE ATTORNEY

ACTEC (The American College of Trust and Estate Counsel) A professional organization of estate attorneys providing a network of seasoned experts. Learn more at actec.org.

Personal Family Lawyer A directory of attorneys who offer a personalized, education-first approach to estate planning. It's ideal for those looking for tailored legal and financial guidance. Learn more at personalfamilylawyer.com.

Note: Although the resources listed above are excellent starting points, many of the attorneys I work with and refer clients to are not found through these channels. I also recommend seeking referrals from trusted friends and colleagues. Ensure that any attorney you consider is properly licensed and specializes in trust and estate law to guarantee the best guidance for your needs.

FUNERAL & MEMORIAL PLANNING

*A **Butterfly Has Been Released*** A powerful documentary from my friends at TGBeyond. Whether you are dealing with a difficult diagnosis yourself, caring for loved ones, or thinking about the future, Allyson's story will resonate with the power of living until the very end, on your own terms. Learn more and watch at tgbeyond.com.

EverLoved Simplifies the planning process by providing a comprehensive online platform for organizing funerals and memorials. I appreciate how it helps families manage everything in one place during tough times. Learn more at everloved.com.

Funeralocity A comparison site for funeral services that helps you find the best options in your area. It's a game-changer for getting transparent pricing and services without the run-around. Learn more at funeralocity.com.

Oaktree Memorials Offers unique, eco-friendly urns and cremation jewelry. Their craftsmanship is top-notch, making them a great choice for honoring a loved one with something beautiful and durable. Learn more at oaktreememorials.com.

GRIEF & CAREGIVER SUPPORT

Help Texts Immediate, expert grief and mental health support via text. Learn more at helptexts.com.

Momento Foundation A non-profit dedicated to creating free grief resources and community tools, supporting teams in the workplace through grief and empathy training, and preserving memories for those facing a terminal diagnosis at no cost to the family. Learn more at momentofoundation.org.

SupportNow Helps supporters provide relief to families in tough times. Gather money, meals, and more in one place. Learn more at supportnow.org.

***When You Can't See the Light: A Trauma-Informed Guide to Surviving a Significant Loss* by Ashley Nicole Jones** A beautiful book and tangible guide to navigating the complexity of grief and loss.

LEARNING MORE ABOUT AFTER LOSS PROFESSIONALS

AfterLight After Loss Professionals Founded by me, AfterLight offers expert after loss and legacy organization services for clients across the U.S. Learn more at myafterlight.com.

Professionals of After Loss Services (PALS) PALS brings together professionals who are passionate about filling the gap in support for families struggling to manage the administrative and logistical tasks of settling an estate while grieving the death of a loved one. Learn more at afterlosspros.com.

LIFE & ESTATE ORGANIZATION

CLEAR Kit Comprehensive Legacy & Estate Organization Made Simple: The CLEAR Kit is your all-in-one solution for organizing and protecting essential estate information with ease and confidence. Available in physical and digital formats. Learn more at shop.buriedinwork.com.

***Family Emergency Handbook: Three Steps to Protect Your Health, Wealth and Loved Ones* by Cindy Arledge** Your step-by-step guide to organizing important documents, communicating decisions, and hosting a family meeting.

LeafPlanner Combines all your estate planning needs into one platform, much like a family office, enhancing decision-making and communication. Learn more at leafplanner.com.

My Data Diary+ Helps compile and organize critical personal and household information in non-cloud-based software. It's like having a digital safety deposit box, but with a one-time fee. Learn more at mydatadiary.com.

Trustworthy's Family Operating System A great tool for securely managing and organizing your family's important documents digitally. I love its user-friendly interface and robust security features. Learn more at trustworthy.com.

PASSWORD MANAGERS

The 6 Best Password Managers (according to Forbes):

NordPass Best browser extension with passkey generation

Dashlane Best password customizations and password health tool

Bitwarden Best affordable open-source solution

1Password Best password manager for beginners

KeePass Best free password manager

Keeper Best multifactor authentication customization

ACKNOWLEDGMENTS

This book has been swirling in my head for years, like a particularly stubborn whirlpool. With each new client and reflective glance back at my personal experiences with death, I felt more inspired and compelled to put pen to paper. I kept talking about writing it until one day, one of my friends, Claudia Calderon, fed up with my procrastination, called my bluff and exclaimed, "Will you shut up already and write it?!" So, I did. And boy, was it hard, but am I ever glad I did, so, thank you Claudia.

A colossal thank you to my husband, Zack, the wind beneath my wings, and the sanity behind my madness. He was there when I declared, "I can't do this!" and was the steadfast voice insisting, "Oh, but you absolutely must!" every step of the way.

To my kids, Finn and Roane: thank you for the space, the silence, and the snacks. Your encouragement and your masterful skill in tiptoeing around the house while I wrote are truly appreciated. Finn, thank you for your understanding when I missed so many of your weekend soccer games because I was writing. Roane, thank you for checking on me and keeping me hydrated with endless refills of my water bottle as I typed away.

To my sister, Randi: thanks for being the official keeper of our childhood's wild tales and details of our shared memories. Thanks for laughing with me through the tough times and for sticking by my side as we survived this circus together.

To Jasmine Hathaway and Mollie Lacher, my partners in this wild, wonderful world of after loss services—thank you for making me a better professional, for your relentless dedication to this work, and for growing this field alongside me. This profession may not come with capes, but if it did, you'd both be rocking them. I'm beyond grateful to be in this with you.

Huge props to the Ripples Media team, especially to Andrew Vogel, who not only believed in me but also supported, tolerated, and, most importantly, helped transform me into an author. When I pitched my idea to you that morning in the coffee shop, I never imagined you'd not only agree to publish my book but also become its most unwavering, enthusiastic supporter. Sometimes, I thought you must be just as crazy as I am. A special shoutout to Lyn Asman as well, who miraculously brought the cover to life and somehow managed not to flee from my requests for "just one tiny change." I truly believe you're a telepathic miracle worker.

Special thanks to Ashley Jones and David Feldman for connecting me with and recommending me to Ripples Media, respectively.

Heartfelt thanks to all my friends—Wendy Patel, Beth Soons, and Jordan Yarbrough for their eagle-eyed proofreading and colleagues, with a special nod to Kristen Rajagopal, who read the draft and provided such insightful and crucial feedback. Gratitude also to Emily Wong and Ella Takieddine for being some of my biggest cheerleaders.

I've never really considered myself an author, and even today, whispering, "I'm an author," feels like I'm sneaking into a club where I don't quite belong. I hope this book helps at least one person because if it does, then I've done my job. If it doesn't, well, at least we had some laughs along the way.

ABOUT THE AUTHOR

Rachel Donnelly might tell you that the cosmos has a quirky sense of humor—handing her a plethora of personal losses at a young age, a "gift" she never asked for. Drowning in grief and chaos initially, Rachel soon decided to turn her heartache into a helping hand. She founded AfterLight, a business dedicated to tackling the ridiculous yet real challenges that arise when someone dies. Through AfterLight, Rachel transforms personal sorrow into supportive solutions, navigating heartfelt and occasionally bizarre stories with her clients.

After years of assisting others and collecting a trove of poignant and sometimes surreal experiences, Rachel felt compelled to put pen to paper. Her book aims to shake up the silence surrounding death, encouraging people to face this uncomfortable topic head-on with proactive conversations. Through her stories, Rachel fosters a new culture of openness about loss and legacy, aiming to transform grief into a shared, connecting human experience.

Rachel is also one of the co-founders of Professionals of After Loss Services (PALS), setting industry standards and creating the After Loss Professional Training Program, an innovative course that molds skilled professionals worldwide. Before diving into the after loss sector, Rachel garnered extensive experience in higher education fundraising, holding roles at institutions like Emory University, Georgia Institute of Technology, and the Shepherd Center Foundation.

An alumna of Agnes Scott College with a B.A. in Political Science, Rachel lives in Atlanta with her husband Zack, their two children, and Rhett Butler, their adorably scheming black lab mix. She believes in facing life's toughest challenges with a blend of sincerity and a touch of wit—because, as she'll tell you, sometimes reality is too absurd to be anything but laughed at.

www.ingramcontent.com/pod-product-compliance
Lightning Source LLC
Chambersburg PA
CBHW040917210326
41597CB00030B/5106